PAS
FOR THE WORK OF
ERICH VON DÄNIKEN

"His ideas have a mythic appeal . . ."

—James A. Herrick, *Christianity Today*

"Erich boldly made us think about what no one else dared to even speak of. He continues to challenge our understanding of history."

—Philip Coppens, author of
The Ancient Alien Question

*"*Chariots of the Gods *is a pivotal book, first published at an important point in human consciousness and awareness, a time when minds were opening. That book changed many others' and my own worldview. Erich von Däniken has again touched the pulse of humanity at another crucial moment in discussing the now known 'fact' that the Gods Never Left Us."*

—Colin Andrews, author of *On the Edge of Reality*

"Erich's newest book is a fascinating journey from the ancient past into the present with a plethora of scientific evidence and documented research. As always, he adds his own 'to the point' take on it all. Readers may also like that his newest work moves in a slightly different direction from his past books. A thoroughly enlightening and enjoyable read."

—Bruce Cunningham, director of Ancient Mysteries International LLC and publisher of *Advanced Archaeology Review* magazine

Confessions *of an* Egyptologist

Confessions *of an* Egyptologist

Lost Libraries, Vanished Labyrinths, and the
Astonishing Truth Under the Saqqara Pyramids

Erich von Däniken
Translated by Bernhard Sulzer

NEW
PAGE

This edition first published in 2021 by New Page Books,
an imprint of

Red Wheel/Weiser, LLC
With offices at:
65 Parker Street, Suite 7
Newburyport, MA 01950
www.redwheelweiser.com

Copyright © 2021 by Erich von Däniken

Translation copyright © 2021 by Bernhard Sulzer

All rights reserved. No part of this publication may be reproduced
or transmitted in any form or by any means, electronic or mechanical, including photocopying, recording, or by any information
storage and retrieval system, without permission in writing from
Red Wheel/Weiser, LLC. Reviewers may quote brief passages.

ISBN: 978-1-63265-191-4

Library of Congress Cataloging-in-Publication Data available upon
request.

Cover design by Kathryn Sky-Peck
Cover illustration © Stefano Bianchetti/Bridgeman Images
Interior photos/images by EvD-Archive, Patrick Wenger, and
        Ramon Zürcher
Interior by Maureen Forys, Happenstance Type-O-Rama
Typeset in ITC New Baskerville, Orpheus Pro, and Franklin Gothic

Printed in the United States of America
IBI
10 9   8 7 6 5 4 3 2 1

TABLE OF CONTENTS

LIST OF ILLUSTRATIONS

Confessions *of an* Egyptologist

CHAPTER 1

The Murder

ON NOVEMBER 17, 1997, an attack took place in front of the Hatshepsut temple in Luxor that resulted in the hideous murder of unarmed tourists by cowardly Islamist psychopaths. The drama started at 9 A.M., as the early November sun burned down on the Nile valley near Luxor. The first tourists were waiting at the ticket booth by Queen Hatshepsut's (1466–1444 BC) temple complex. They had come to marvel at the unique grave site. Information above the little window showed the current admission prices, and to the left was a copy of an engraving from the temple that read: "Built as a monument to Amun, Lord of the Two Thrones. Amun is the Most Holy One."

Suddenly, six young bearded Arabs stood in front of the ticket clerk, who looked up in astonishment, expecting them to ask about tickets. Then one of the six men opened his jacket, pulled out a Kalashnikov and shot the clerk and two inspectors standing next to him, killing all three.

The tourists in the queue started to scatter, but it was too late. Whole groups of them were simply mowed down. Even after forty minutes, there was neither a policeman nor any military personnel on the premises. No siren sounded; no military helicopter appeared. The cold-blooded killers had a free hand to target individuals or groups who were trying to escape or hide. The echo of the victims' screams rang from the temple walls to the rocky sides of the valley that enclosed the site.

When they were done shooting, the terrorists began massacring their victims with machetes—all in the name of Allah. They placed a message praising Islam in the hacked-open body of a Japanese visitor. A five-year-old British boy and a couple on their honeymoon were also slaughtered. A forty-five-year-old woman from Freiburg (Switzerland) threw herself protectively over her daughter, held her tight, and closed her eyes. But when the rattle of the automatic weapons finally stopped, blood flowed from the child's face. Murdered. Twenty-three-year-old Manuela Kamuf from Lörrach pretended to be dead, lying beside her father, Karl-Heinz. Several shots had ripped his face apart.

The result of this horror? Fifty-eight tourists dead, including thirty-six Swiss, ten Japanese, six British, four German, and two Colombian. In addition, four Egyptians—three police officers and a tour guide—were killed.

That tour guide was my friend, Adel H., and this book is about him.

Adel and I were friends who had shared a great deal of knowledge about some of Egypt's millennia-old secrets—those under the Saqqara pyramid and those under the Sphinx. On many nights, we had talked about the administrators within the Egyptian civil-service hierarchy and their connections to archaeologists. Adel let me know in no uncertain terms that he shouldn't be having these conversations—especially not with me. He counted on my discretion. Over twenty years have passed since Adel's murder.

On that fateful morning, Adel accompanied a group of Swiss tourists from the Hotel Meridian in Luxor to the boat that would take them across the Nile and then, on the other side of the river, to the modern, air-conditioned bus that would carry them to the mortuary temple. As I later learned from a survivor, the mood on board was relaxed and friendly. Everyone was looking forward to seeing Queen Hatshepsut's temple, which stood directly at the bottom of the steep rock face of the Theban Desert mountains.

Adel prepared his group for their experience by giving them some background and history over the bus's loudspeakers. Hatshepsut, he told them, had ruled Egypt for twenty years. Illustrations and statues show her as a stately figure dressed in male robes with a beard and the insignia of the ruler. But Hatshepsut was, in fact, a woman (see Figure 1). Was she the world's first transgender person? It's possible.

Figure 1. The mortuary temple of Hatshepsut, located on the west bank of the Nile near the Valley of the Kings.

When Pharaoh Thutmosis II, of the Eighteenth Dynasty, died in 1479 BC, his son Thutmosis III (1486–1425 BC) should have inherited the throne, but he was still a child. His stepmother, Hatshepsut, ascended the throne instead and eventually had herself crowned pharaoh. She also created a myth about her alleged divine origin, claiming that she had been created by the god Amun. After her death, the rightful heir, Thutmosis III, finally became pharaoh and ruled for thirty-three years.

Adel explained to the tourists that the temple they would arrive at in a few minutes was one of the greatest achievements of the New Kingdom. The architects who had worked there millennia ago had created a structure that consisted of three harmoniously layered terraces. Hatshepsut probably chose the location because, centuries earlier, a sanctuary of Hathor, goddess of fertility, love, art, and science, had stood there.

The temple itself was built at the end a kilometer-long processional road that had originally been flanked on both sides by stone sphinxes. This avenue of sphinxes had once led beyond this temple site to the Amun-Re site in Karnak, over twelve kilometers away in a straight line. These sphinxes were hybrid beings, like the famous Sphinx in front of the Great Pyramid, the largest of its type. Today, tourists can still walk a three-kilometer sphinx-lined avenue that connects the temples of Luxor and Karnak.

The temple of Hatshepsut is intersected by a sloping ramp that connects the second of its three terraces with the third (see color insert). At the end of the ramp on the third terrace, there are twelve columns on each side. Behind them, on the temple wall, reliefs survive that depict scenes from a distant past. One shows a trip from the Nile to the mysterious land of Punt. Another tells the story of the creation of Hatshepsut by the god Amun. Yet another portrays the facial features of Hatshepsut herself, with a painted beard and the insignia of royalty. According to Adel, two statues of the god Osiris, each five and a half meters tall, originally stood in front of the pillars of the top terrace. Queen Hatshepsut herself appears in nine colossal statues and no fewer than twenty-six smaller ones. The temple is truly a monument for eternity.

The tourist bus reached the site's parking lot at 9:12 A.M. Adel asked the members of his group to reassemble at the same place in two hours. He stayed at the bus door until the last guests had left the vehicle. As his tourist group crossed the 200 meters between the parking lot and the ticket booth, Adel heard the first shots. He ran past his group, saw one of the killers with his Kalashnikov, and shouted something at him in Arabic—probably "What are you doing?" or "In the name of Allah, stop!" One survivor told me that the terrorist merely grinned, then raised his gun and blasted his countryman and fellow believer, Adel, away with several shots.

The authorities later revealed which terrorist group had committed this act, who had trained them, and who was behind it. I didn't care anymore. When their heinous attack subsided, the terrorists stole a bus and continued their murderous rampage at the next temple, where an exchange of gun fire with police ensued. One of the attackers was shot; the others escaped into a cave. There, encircled by the army that had, by that time, moved in, they reportedly committed suicide.

Personally, I don't believe a word of it. The security forces wiped out the terrorists as they cowered in that cave because their statements would not have been allowed to be aired in any court in the land or revealed to the world at large. These assassins had defiled the name of Allah. They would have told lies in the name of Allah. Clearly, these deluded murderers didn't even know their own holy book, the Koran. If they had, they would have known that Allah, who is worshipped several times a day, does not need the help of murderers to enforce his will.

Surah 2 verse 118 of the holy book tells us: "If Allah wants something, he only thinks it is, and it will happen." If Allah didn't want tourists visiting Egypt or didn't want his faith and its monuments shared with non-believers, he would only have to think "so it is," and immediately, so it would be. To think that Allah is so small and powerless that he needs the help of fanatics is an insult to the grand creator.

What troubles me is that well-known mullahs never come before their believers after a gross act of violence committed in Allah's name and make it unmistakably clear that Allah does not condone murder, that those who support or commit assassinations are never acting in his name. The world has, in fact, become immersed in these lies—particularly with regard to religion.

CHAPTER 2

First Encounter

OUR IMAGINATIONS ARE INTRIGUED by civilizations that flourished millennia ago. Why? Because the
writings of these cultures either no longer exist or are
slumbering in secret archives somewhere. Archeology
succeeds in bringing some order and understanding to
this distant past, but with that order new questions arise.
Today, we know that, to date, only about 20 percent of all
Egyptian antiquities have been excavated.

But how many of us are aware that there are chambers under the Great Pyramid of Giza? Or that new shafts,
chambers, and corridors are located and electronically
measured every year in the same pyramid? Or that the
so-called "pyramid texts" from the Second and Third
Dynasties of Egypt tell us, not only about the wishes of
a pharaoh for the afterlife, but also about actual space

flights by ancient rulers? Or that the Egyptians mummified myriad animals, including millions of birds and hundreds of thousands of crocodiles, bulls, hippos, and snakes, as well as smaller creatures like beetles, scorpions, rats, and fish?

How many are aware that the ancient Egyptians, those who lived 2,500 or more years ago, did not themselves know who built the Great Pyramid? Or that Caliph Abdullah al-Ma'mun, the first to enter the pyramid in 832 AD after it had been sealed for thousands of years, discovered inside it the body of a human-like being wearing armor made of an unknown metal, along with strange stones and unidentifiable objects?

These questions are perplexing. But even more perplexing is that these facts are not publicly known. Egypt is open to tourists; anyone can travel there and be astonished by what they see. That's why I take small groups of curious people there every few years, hoping that they will become enlightened and pursue more knowledge about Egypt's ancient civilization. And, of course, every study group is accompanied by a trained expert in Egyptology. And that's how I first met Adel H. in the fall of 1981.

THE CONVERSATION BEGINS

Adel introduced himself as I rode the bus to my hotel. He was humble, not intrusive—a lean, tall figure with somber facial features and black hair. Unlike most Egyptians, he had no beard or mustache. His teeth were well-maintained and his smile was natural. He didn't try to overwhelm tourists with unnecessary talk and arrogance, and he never tried to force knowledge on them in which they weren't interested. He just patiently answered their questions. He knew Egypt and its people and instructed us competently about the laws and religions of the Nile region. Although Muslim, he drank red wine with his guests in small sips.

As I got to know Adel, I asked him who had assigned him to our group. Did tour guides have any kind of governing body that decided who would lead a specific group?

"I wanted to have this group," Adel replied. "My wish was to meet you." He looked me straight in the eye. There was a tourist office somewhere in Cairo, he told me, with a canteen for the tour guides. Incoming parties were listed on a large message board, along with information like arrival and departure dates, number of participants, tour operator, category (boat or bus trip? moderate? luxurious?), language, average age of participants, etc. When he saw my name listed with one group, he ran straight to his supervisor to request that he lead our tour. The supervisor stared at him for a long time and finally asked whether he knew who I was, warning him that I had a reputation for being quite well informed and for contradicting the local travel guides. Adel told his boss that he knew of my books and was not afraid of my possible know-it-all attitude any more than he was bothered by the uninformed questions of the other tour members.

"Where did you learn to speak German so perfectly?" I asked him, after he had explained.

"I studied for four years at the Institute for Egyptology at the University of Vienna," Adel replied. "I also studied epigraphy, German, and of course hieroglyphic texts and monuments. And, believe it or not," he went on, "I actually attended one of your lectures at the university. You even signed one of your books for me. But you will probably not remember that."

On subsequent evenings, usually after the tourists had retired to their quarters, Adel and I often met at the bar in the Hotel Semiramis, which is not far from the pyramids. Slowly, I began to realize why Adel was interested in me. He saw in me a theoretician, a bookworm, who had access to ancient texts. He, on the other hand, was a practitioner. He dug in the field, crawled into abandoned shafts, and also worked with grave robbers. When I expressed my surprise that a legitimate Egyptologist and officially recognized tour guide would work with grave robbers, he told me about the relationships that existed between the Razuls, a long-established grave-robber clan, and the archaeological community. In fact, in the fall of 1922, it was young Ahmed Razul who led British archeologist Howard Carter (1874–1939) to the burial chamber of Tutankhamun. When Adel inquired if I knew the story of Howard Carter, I replied that I was familiar with only the barest details of his work.

"What you know is probably just the public version," Adel said with a smile. "Howard Carter wasn't the innocent academic we know from the textbooks. He had worked as an inspector of the antiquity administration for Upper Egypt and Nubia since 1899 and, during this time, also worked with grave robbers." Carter probably couldn't have made his historic discovery in any other way, Adel claimed, because professional archeology was just emerging as a legitimate field at the time. In fact, from 1904 to 1908, Carter worked as a painter, a tourist guide, and an interpreter in Luxor, during which time he received antiquities from the Razuls and sold them to tourists.

"Carter returned to Luxor from England in late October 1922," Adel continued, "armed with the financial support of a wealthy Englishman, Lord Carnarvon (1866–1923). In early November, as Carter was excavating the tomb of Ramses VI in the Valley of the Kings (see color insert), he came across a cartouche of the god Anubis and sent a telegram about it to his sponsor in London. I know the text from my time at the university," Adel reported:

> *Made at last wonderful discovery in the Valley, a magnificent tomb with seals intact, recovered same for your arrival. I have it sealed again for your arrival.*

But that telegram was a lie, Adel insisted, smiling in a forgiving way and sipping his wine. Ahmed Razul, one of the sons of the grave-robber family, had actually led Howard Carter to this tomb days *earlier*

After receiving this telegram, Carter's sponsor, Lord Carnarvon, promptly traveled to Egypt and together, before the eyes of journalists and some experts, they presided over an official opening of the tomb. Witnesses reported at the time that some workers pushed stone slabs to the side and Carter held a torch into a crack. The anxious Lord Carnarvon, standing behind him, couldn't wait any longer and asked impatiently: "What do you see?"

Carter replied calmly: "I see incredible things."

"But, again, Carter was lying," Adel asserted. "He had been in the tomb days earlier, led by Ahmed Razul. He probably took some treasures so he would not have to share them with the government." When I asked why he would do that, Adel responded that Carter's agreement obliged him to leave half of the treasures to the Egyptians. And he wanted his share. An inventory of the find taken years later showed that there were exactly 5,398 objects in Tutankhamun's tomb—the best known being the young king's golden death mask, which is shown today in special exhibitions around the world. The incredible story that Adel told me back in 1981 was confirmed five years later by Egyptologist Dr. Rolf Krauss.[1]

Howard Carter lost his interest in scientific archeology after the discovery of Tutankhamun's tomb. He no longer wanted to have anything to do with the antiquities administration in Cairo, and he often scolded them publicly. He went on to earn a livelihood from lectures and juicy commissions as an art dealer. He died of a lung disease on March 2, 1939, at his home in Kensington, England. Journalists at the time wrote of "a curse of the pharaohs."

Considering Adel's revelation that the most famous discoverer of Egyptian antiquities—one of the world's most admired archaeologists—was, in fact, a grave robber, I shook my head in dismay.

"I'm an Egyptologist and tour guide as well," Adel countered, "and I can't get anywhere without the grave robbers. For better or worse, they are a part of our society."

"Have you ever sold real antiquities?" I enquired.

"Yes," he replied. "I couldn't do it any other way."

"So you know tombs that have not yet been discovered archeologically?"

"Not only that," he assured me. "My family knows of spacious underground structures that must date from a time so far back that we can't even grasp it. Tens of thousands of years ago or more."

I did not contradict him, but instead asked if I could possibly see at least parts of these structures. I explained to him that I was familiar with some ancient books that were written 2,000 or more years ago that reported on the existence of underground labyrinths. The ancient authors even talked about the age of these labyrinths, placing them so far back in time as to amaze and puzzle today's archaeologists. And I couldn't help but wonder under which deserts, settlements, or sanctuaries these labyrinths might be hidden. Where were these lost, underground worlds from distant times? Had they been excavated and then covered up again? If so, by whom? Had these long-forgotten structures become inaccessible due to natural disasters?

And where are the millions of books that were written in that distant past? Were they burned? Damaged?

Deliberately destroyed? And if so, again, why? Is the little that we see today all that there is? Or do secret libraries exist, accessible only to hooded guards or members of obscure orders? Who actually had an interest in writing, hoarding, and then hiding books for millennia? Who wanted to make these books disappear again? Did Adel actually know of lost libraries? Had the clan of grave robbers discovered chambers or even halls filled with treasures that were thousands of years old and remained silent about them? Was Adel an initiate of one of these groups? And, if so, why was he sharing this knowledge with me?

KINDRED SPIRITS

In March 1984, I invited Adel and his wife to spend two weeks with me in Switzerland, where we spent many afternoons in my archive, of which I am very proud. It houses over 100,000 pictures that are neatly organized and stored in drawers, along with my correspondence with famous and lesser-known people from all over the world.

One afternoon as we pored over my collection seated at my conference table, sipping strong black tea and smoking, I asked Adel: "Why are there no Arabic versions of any of my books?" I showed him translations of my work into Chinese, Japanese, Tamil, Russian, and of course English, French, and Spanish. "What do the Arabs have against me?"

"I don't think they have anything against you," Adel replied. "They don't know anything about you. It is rather the Islamic clergy who condemn your works."

"But why? I make it clear in every book that I am a deeply religious person."

"But in your books, you write about *gods*—plural," Adel pointed out. "This is not at all compatible with the Koran. Think of the prayers that are sung six times a day from the minaret: "*La ilahe allallah Muhammeden rasulullah*" ("Allah is great and Mohammed is his prophet"). There must be no gods besides Allah.

"But my so-called 'gods' aren't gods at all," I protested. "In fact, there are no gods. We know that today, although our Stone Age ancestors didn't." I explained that our ancestors viewed extraterrestrials as deities, and that was how the belief in "gods" came about. "Everything is just a huge misunderstanding!" I exclaimed. "The 'gods' were, in fact, extraterrestrial astronauts."

"You don't have to explain that to *me*," laughed Adel. "But try to convince the Muslim clergy!"

We later decided that Adel should translate one of my books from German into High Arabic to increase the chance that an Arab publishing house might become interested in my work. Adel worked diligently on this project and the translation was completed six months later. But we still couldn't find a buyer. Adel spoke to several academic and intellectually curious publishers, including some who had studied in the West. But nobody wanted to take the risk. Everyone was afraid of the mullahs, who feared a kind of "spiritual revolution"—an uprising by the faithful against the holy Koran. Although I decried this attitude, I understood it very well. After all, I was familiar with the long, painful history of the destruction of millions of books.

As Adel and I pondered these difficult subjects, I realized that I had found in Adel a kindred spirit and a fellow investigator. And that was when I decided that I would pass on to him all the knowledge that I had collected over decades and published in stages in previous books. And Adel's curiosity and amazement only increased in the telling. What do we actually know, we asked each other, about the unknown writers who worked millennia ago and the legacy they may have left?

GIFTS FROM THE GODS

The entire history of our intellectual past began with the awakening of the mind. Our former monkey-like ancestors communicated through grunts and hisses. Then they developed language, which, according to my research, arose from a targeted, artificial mutation brought forth by extraterrestrials visiting the Earth. Science rejects this theory, however, and claims that language evolved through natural changes. At some point in the process, people learned to count using their fingers and toes, placing stones together in groups to denote larger quantities of animals and goods. At about this time, humans began building temples and priests began demanding sacrifices, which had to be tallied as well.

After rudimentary language and the ability to count, humans developed pictorial signs—today known as pictograms—to express more complicated thoughts and meanings. Then, as early as the fourth millennium BC, abstract signs emerged from wedge-shaped marks that combined to create the first written language—cuneiform.

The largest cuneiform library found to date is that of King Ashurbanipal, who ruled the Assyrian Empire from 669 to 631 BC. His huge collection was found in the 19th century in the hills of Kujundshik near the former city of Nineveh, now in northern Iraq near Mosul. During his reign, Ashurbanipal had no fewer than 25,000 clay tablets inscribed, each of which contained his name. These include a copy of the *Epic of Gilgamesh*, a Babylonian creation myth known as the *Enuma Elish*, and a copy of the *Codex Hammurabi*, a collection of laws that the Babylonia king Hammurabi (1728–1686 BC) had ordered chiseled on stone tablets that made explicit reference to "divine revelations."[2]

Ashurbanipal, who ruled around 1,000 years after Hammurabi, must have been a very learned ruler. He had older texts from distant libraries copied by his own scribes and brought to Nineveh, and also confiscated entire clay-tablet collections on his military campaigns. He prided himself on being able to write and claimed to be familiar with the science of reading signs in the sky. He also claimed to know the writings from before the time of the great flood.

Contrary to current scientific views that cuneiform writing developed over a millennia-long process, the learned writers of the time report something different.

They claim the script was given to mankind by the gods. Diodorus of Sicily, who lived in the first century BC and spent several years in Alexandria, writes that people first "lived in a disorderly and semi-animalistic state."[3] They searched for food independently and only worked together when they were attacked by wild animals. At first, their language consisted of a variety of different sounds, but they gradually learned to assign certain sounds (words) to certain objects.

During this period of human development, the gods suddenly arrived and encouraged humans to give up their primitive means of survival and instructed them in the skills of mining, agriculture, and husbandry. They taught them how to grow wheat and barley, and how to raise certain animals as a source of food in lean times. Lastly, the gods gave "a lot of names to things for which no name was known." And then they taught a few people to write.

Several of the ancient writers, including Berossos, a priest of Babylon who lived in the fourth century BC, agree with Diodorus's interpretation of the early development of human society. Berossos wrote a three-volume history called the *Babyloniaca*, of which only a few original fragments remain. We owe what little we know of this critical early work to descriptions by Alexander Polyhistor (c. 100 BC), church dignitary Eusebius of Caesarea (260–339 AD), and Jewish historian Flavius Josephus (37–c. 100 AD). According to surviving portions of the work, Berossos tells of how humans were originally instructed by gods:

> *In the first year, an intelligent creature with the name Oannes*
> *arose out of the Eritrean Sea [today the Arabian Sea]. This*
> *creature spent the daytime with people without eating and*
> *passed on its knowledge of writing, science and other arts to*
> *them and taught them how to build cities and temples, how to*
> *introduce laws and how to survey the land . . . Since that time,*
> *people have not learned anything that is significantly new.[4]*

Depending on the translation, Oannes is interpreted as "fish creature," "wise man," or "scholar." It is astonishing that a similar teacher named Yma appears in the holy book of the Parsi, the *Avesta*.[5] And even old Chinese traditions speak of a heavenly teacher who brought writing to people.[6] Japanese creation myths include similar descriptions.[7]

In fact, ancient historians across many cultures reported that it was the gods who taught people to write. In the fifth volume of his lengthy history, the bishop and historian Eusebius reports on the Chaldeans:

> *And in the first year, a terrible monster arose from the Ara-*
> *bian Sea, in the middle of the Babylonian region . . . with*
> *the voice of a human, whose image and drawing are still*
> *kept . . . the same animal spent its day with the humans*
> *without eating any kind of food . . . and it taught people*
> *writing and the various arts.[8]*

But whether language and writing were gifts from the gods or the product of evolution, hundreds of thousands of volumes were created in the ancient world. In Egypt, these were written in hieroglyphs, which first appeared as early as 3200 BC in the so-called "prince's tomb" of Naquada III. This form of writing, which originally developed out of an earlier pictorial script, made use of nearly 7,000 hieroglyphic characters by around 600 BC. In fact, the word "hieroglyph" means "sacred character" in ancient Greek, and the Egyptians themselves called their hieroglyphs "script of the godly words." According to their tradition, it was Thoth, the god of wisdom, who taught them the script.

ANCIENT ARCHIVES

The Egyptians wrote on everything—temple walls, pillars, ceilings, and even deep inside the pyramids. There, for example in the tomb of Unas (2356–2323 BC), the walls were completely covered with inscriptions.

In an important step forward, the Egyptians discovered how to tranfer the content of their stone tablets to sheets of papyrus, a water plant whose individual stems can grow up to four meters tall. The plant's green bark is removed from the stems with a knife and cut into strips about twenty centimeters long. In the past, sandals, belts, and small handbags were made from this bark. Today, the waste is used as a fuel. The pulp inside the stems is cut into *lamellas,* or strips, and placed in a water bath for six days to saturate the strips and turn them brown. Then the strips are squeezed with a press or rolling pin and placed in a cross-hatched pattern on a cotton cloth. These cross-hatched strips and cloths are layered and stored until they are completely dry. Because the papyrus pulp contains gelatin, the dried strips stick together, forming what we know as a sheet of papyrus. After about a week, the cross-hatched sections become an elastic and quite resilient sheet that can be written on easily and painted in all colors.

With the invention of papyrus, the number of written documents grew rapidly. Indeed, entire libraries of papyrus documents were created, the best known being the great library at Alexandria, while palm-leaf libraries grew from an analogous process developed in Asia. Today, inscribed papyrus sheets are sold as souvenirs for tourists because they can be transported easily, do not break, and can be framed and hung in any room as mementoes of the mysterious land on the Nile.

In a parallel development that took place around 400 BC, scribes in what was Pergamon (now Bergama, in western Turkey) began using parchment made from processed animal skins to record documents. No fewer than 200,000 parchment scrolls are said to have been kept at Pergamon alone. In fact, the Pergamon collection grew to become the second largest library in the world at that time, as reported by Strabo (c. 63 BC–23 AD) in his work *Geographica*. Strabo wrote that Eumenes II (221–158 BC), the king of Pergamon, had enlarged the city with monuments and a large library, although the location of this site remained hidden for over 1,500 years, until German engineer Carl Humann (1839–1896) accidentally came across ruins on the southern slope of the city of Bergama. He was commissioned by the Deutsche Museum in Berlin to carry out excavations at the site, which he led from 1876 to 1886. Humann gained great fame as an archaeologist through these excavations, and Pergamon became a center of German antiquity research, as attested to by the magnificent collections in the Pergamon Museum in Berlin.

On the other side of the Mediterranean Sea, in Egypt, Ptolemy I ruled from 367 to 282 BC. Ptolemy was originally a general under Alexander the Great (356–323 BC). After Alexander's death, he secured power in Egypt and founded the Ptolemaic dynasties. He must have been a learned person, because he founded the famous library of Alexandria, turning the former seaside resort into an intellectual Mecca. World-famous scholars like Euclid (the father of geometry, c. 300 BC), Archimedes (the greatest mathematician of the time, 287–212 BC), and Diodorus of Sicily (historian of the first century BC) studied in the library at Alexandria. At the time of Julius Caesar (c. 47 BC), the library was said to have contained an astounding 700,000 papyrus rolls and parchments.

During these epochs, every reigning dynasty in the world had a library—take, for instance, the kings and queens of Saba, which comprises modern-day Ethiopia and Yemen. Even cultures in distant Central America valued the written word and collected documents of all kinds in archives and libraries. The Maya painted tens of thousands of leaves with four-color drawings, calling them "codices" (plural of "codex"). The individual pages are made of thin layers of the bark of the fig tree. The bark was first tapped flat and then rendered flexible with the sap of the rubber tree. After being made stronger by applying starch from plant tubers, the finished sheets were laid on a flat stone and covered with an extremely thin layer of lime, which helped to bring out the colors. Finally, a thin, transparent varnish was applied over the finished painted sheet. The Maya inscribed their leaves on both sides and finally glued the individual leaves together on one edge, effectively creating a binding. Mayan writings can be pulled apart like a hand organ (see Figure 2). Overall, the Maya used no fewer than 6,730 main characters and 7,500 so-called "affixes," or added syllables, in their writing.

Thomas Barthel, a Mayan researcher, found that the Mayan script was "overtly variable" because the same characters can mean completely different things.[9] According to Barthel, there are also "whole blocks of hieroglyphs that occur in the middle of a number text," as well as word games "that offer numerous reading variants whose meanings point in very different directions."[10] In fact, the jungle of Mayan hieroglyphs is so dense that only a few experts take it on. Probably the best Maya epigraphers (typeface experts) are David and George Stuart from the University of Texas at Austin. In their most recent publication, they analyzed the characters found on the famous grave plate of Palenque and came away with completely new insights.[11]

Previous interpretations had taken the characters to mean that the Mayan ruler Pakal plunged into the open throat of a monster, and that the "cross of life" grew out of his chest. These fanciful interpretations are all nonsense, the Stuarts claim. Their analysis, in fact, shows something quite different: "Viewed as a whole, the plate can be seen as a conscientiously constructed model of the cosmos."[12]

What seems so puzzling to researchers today, however, is probably due to intentional obfuscation by the Maya. Their holy books were considered a secret code, intended only for priests and initiates. In addition, the language and pictorial forms in these documents differed between tribal areas, just as the dialects of modern languages do today. Today, we know of more than 1,200 Mayan writings, although some are only fragments that have been excavated at over a hundred sites. In addition to these, we find writings on Mayan temples and staircases. In fact, "all temples are littered with characters and images," notes Mayan archaeologist Herbert Wilhelmy.[13]

Figure 2. Mayan codex.

But if these monumental collections of ancient writings and books existed in all parts of the world—thousands, tens of thousands, hundreds of thousands, millions of writings—where did they go? In addition to the libraries that survived and were made accessible to everyone who knew how to read—even then, millennia ago!—were other secret libraries built? And if so, why? Was it out of fear that enemies would destroy them?

LOST LIBRARIES

I believe that these libraries were hidden, not because of a fear of enemies, but rather because a catastrophic flood was foretold, one that the "elders" anticipated because of their knowledge of an earlier flood. Plato's account of Atlantis, for instance, tells of the annihilations of several earlier human civilizations:

> *In order to get them to tell him about the prehistoric times, he once spoke about the oldest times in Greece . . . and Niobe, and how after the great flood Deucalion and Pyrrha remained . . . And just as writing and everything else otherwise required by urban culture had been established, the great flood of the heavens engulfs the world again like a disease and only sees those people survive who do not understand anything about writing and are completely uneducated. So it happens that you always become young again and again, without any information about what happened in the old times, be it here at our time or in your time . . . Because you only remember one flood of the Earth whilst there have been so many before.* [14]

As I pointed out in a previous book, stories of a great flood appear everywhere in ancient literature.[15] A multitude of authors across many cultures and in many locations tell of a catastrophic flood that occurred in ancient times. The Greek geographer Strabo (c. 63 BC–23 AD), Pliny the Elder (23–79 AD), Hesiod (c. 700 BC), Herodotus (486–430 BC), Hekataios (550–480 BC), the Babylonian Berossos (late fourth and early third centuries BC), Diodorus of Sicily (first century BC), the Phoenician Sanchuniathon (c. 150 BC), and many unknown Mayan writers all wrote about great floods that occurred 10,000 or more years ago.

I contend that these floods were the reason why hidden libraries were created, so that posterity might never forget what the ancestors had known. In his *Chronicle*, Eusebius tells us how Kron "gave orders to bury and put away all written works, both the first and the last, in the Sun City of Sipur."[16] And, in fact, I contend that the Great Pyramid at Giza is nothing more than a huge library, erected before the flood to preserve the knowledge of the time. I base this on my knowledge of the ancient texts.

The prophet Enoch, for example, whom I have discussed several times and who lived before the flood, wrote that he had authored over a hundred works and had given them to his son Methuselah before his "ascension." Why?

And now my son Methuselah . . . I have revealed everything to you and have given you the books which concern all these

*things. Preserve, my son Methuselah, the books written by
your father's hand and deliver them to the coming generations after the flood.*[17]

Which books? And what would they have to do with the
Great Pyramid?

According to the myths of the Jews of prehistoric times,
Enoch was "a king over men, who lived 243 years."[18] In the
first book of Moses, he appears as the seventh of the ten
founding fathers—one of the patriarchs who ruled *before*
the flood (Genesis 5: 21ff). He was the first person to leave
the Earth in a fiery chariot (a spaceship?) and was brought
into heaven by angels (extraterrestrials?), where he learned
to write. He was given a "quick-writing tool" and an angel
named Vrevoel dictated scientific works to him.

*And the Lord called one of his archangels named Vrevoel . . .
and he said to Vrevoel: Bring out the books and take a writing tool and give it to Enoch and show him the books. And
Vrevoel hurried and brought the books to me and handed me
the fast-writing tool . . . And Vrevoel was reciting to me all
the works of Heaven and Earth and of the sea and all elements. About animals, thunder, the sun and the moon and
the stars and their cycles and changes and times and years
and days and hours. And the rising of the clouds and winds.*

That was followed by more teachings about physics and
engineering.

How do we know all this? Because Enoch, in addition
to his scientific works—all of which were deposited in the

Great Pyramid—also wrote the *Book of Enoch*, in which he told about himself and his experiences. This book was discovered by Scottish traveler James Bruce (1730–1794) in a monastery library in Abyssinia and brought to London in 1773.[19] Here we learn that it was Enoch who gave the order to build the Great Pyramid—before the flood, having been given his engineering skills by the angels, extraterrestrials.

All this can be read in the *Hitat*, a work by geographer and historian Taqi al-Din Ahmad ibn Ali ibn Abd al-Qadir ibn Muhammad al-Maqrizi (1364–1442):

> ... *the first Hermes* ... *it is the one the Hebrews call Enoch, son of Jared, son of Mahalalel, son of Kenan, son of Enos, son of Seth, son of Adam* ... *He read in the stars that the great flood would come. Then he had the pyramids built and filled them with treasures, scholarly writings and everything he thought could be lost and disappear, in order to keep things safe.*[20]

But *which* treasures are actually in the pyramids? Al-Maqrizi continues:

> ... *they were filled with devices and statues made of precious stones, with devices made of excellent iron-like weapons that don't rust, with glass that can be folded up without breaking, with strange talismans* ... *in the eastern pyramid. He had the vaults of heaven and the planets depicted and had paintings made that portray what his ancestors had created. Incense was added, which was sacrificed to the stars and books about the stars.*

> *You can also find the fixed stars there and certain occur-*
> *rences during their life cycle . . . there wasn't any science*
> *that he could not put into words and record. He also had the*
> *treasures of the stars and the prophets brought there, and they*
> *formed a huge and uncountable amount.* [21]

Clear enough?

The *Hitat* also relates that "God" personally instructed Enoch in astronomy and made it known to him that a catastrophe would come over the Earth. This assertion is corroborated by the discovery that Caliph Abdallah Al-Ma'mun made in the pyramid in 832, after it had been closed for thousands of years. He reports finding a sarcophagus depicting a human-like creature that wore armor made of an unknown metal. In addition, he reports discovering strange shining stones and other unidentifiable objects.

As Adel pondered all I had told him over a glass of wine, he commented that he thought it unlikely that the ancients would have known anything about a global flood.

"Unless someone warned them," I countered. "And who could have warned them? Moreover the hidden books in the Great Pyramid are not an isolated case. There were hidden libraries all over the world. Take, for instance, *The Book of Mormon*," I said, crossing over to the bookshelf and handing Adel a copy. "This tells the story of a religious group called the Mormons who are now based in Salt Lake City, in the United States. It also describes how the forefathers of the Mormons inscribed thousands and thousands of metal plates—not stone, not parchment, not papyrus. The plates had to be metal so they could survive the ravages of time. On these plates, the Mormon forefathers recorded all knowledge, beginning with Adam and covering all of man's time on Earth. Then they hid this metal library, preserving the knowledge for their descendants living in the distant future."

"And where is this treasure today?" Adel asked. I opened the *Book of Mormon* to chapter 8 (verses 16ff), and read:

> *Blessed is he who brings these things to light; for they will be revealed according to God's Word; yes, they will be brought out of the Earth, shine through the darkness and become known to the people . . . and nobody can prevent it. And they will appear on a day when it will be said that miracles have ceased; and it will be as if someone is talking about the dead . . . yes, it will happen on a day when you will hear of fire, storms and smoke fumes in distant lands. You will also hear of wars and rumors of war and earthquakes in various locations.*

"Eerie!" Adel whispered, looking fearfully around him, seemingly in awe. "Do we live in this time?"

"We're moving toward it," I said slowly. "It seems to me that the time of knowledge is fast approaching. Maybe another forty or fifty years? Who knows, maybe you or someone from the Razul family will bring these treasures to light. Think of the prophecy I just read: 'Blessed is he who brings these things to light.'"

SECRET ROOMS

In May 1985, I again spent a few days with Adel. This time we stayed in the Mena House Hotel, which has stood at the end of "Pyramid Road" since 1886. Many famous people have stayed there, from the Prince of Wales to Winston Churchill, from Jimmy Carter to crime writer Agatha Christie. Adel and I dined and chatted in the pleasant restaurant, interrupted only by soft piano music playing in the background. Later, at the bar, Adel said that he was tired and dissatisfied with his work, not because of the tourists—they were all bearable—but because of the antiquities administration. New orders were being given out all the time.

"What orders?" I asked.

Adel replied under his breath: "Things that we should convey to the tourists, but which are not correct at all." I didn't pursue what he said then, but I decided that, at some point in the evening, I would question him about whether he had ever crawled into any underground libraries in the course of his grave-robbing career. When I finally did ask him, he fidgeted on his bar stool and lit a cigarette.

"Egypt is a country with a known history and an unknown history," he began hesitantly "and the unknown one is much older than we all imagine. New rooms and corridors are discovered every year. Over eighty years ago, in the autumn of 1933, an excavator named Selim Hassan came across a shaft directly under the ramp to the pyramid of Chephren. Because of the groundwater, he did not get any farther than fifteen meters into the rock. Twelve years later, Egyptologist Abdel-Moneim Abu-Bakr followed a side tunnel that ran from the original shaft toward the pyramid of Cheops and found several chambers to the right and left of it. Today, they are looted. I don't know what was inside. Then a few brothers of the Razul clan managed to drain some of the groundwater," he continued, "an arduous job, because the pump failed every time and the water seeped in again."

Adel paused as if to gather his courage, then continued. "Erich," he said, spreading his arms as if to wrap them around me, "down there lies a sarcophagus covered with crystal-clear water. The lid probably weighs a few tons and it is carved with incredible precision. The lid is pushed aside slightly, and the sarcophagus itself is empty. But we know with absolute certainty that several shafts run in various directions from that underground chamber."

Well, needless to say, I was intrigued by these revelations, and I never forgot this conversation, although I suspected that I may have misheard some of Adel's description. Then, about twenty years later, Zahi Hawass, then director of the antiquities administration, publicly claimed that he had discovered this same shaft—even though the real discoverer had been Selim Hassan. The shaft had, in fact, been known since 1933 and confirmed by excavations carried out by Egyptologist Abdel-Moneim Abu-Bakr in 1945.

Moreover, it had long been known that there were several sarcophagi down there. And now the eloquent Zahi Hawass, who likes to pretend to be Egypt's Indiana Jones, was claiming that he had personally discovered the shaft and that it contained bones from the Twenty-Sixth Dynasty (663–525 BC). Unbelievable! To make things worse, Hawass announced that he had ordered examinations deep in the shaft that yielded spectacular results. Red-painted ceramic pieces from the Sixth Dynasty (!) had also been found deep down in the chamber. This would make the underground system around 2,000 years older than the Twenty-Sixth Dynasty, otherwise these ceramics could not have been found there.

The entrance to this underground world leads four meters down into a kind of anteroom. From there, a 13.25-meter vertical shaft leads into a room that contains seven niches. Five of these are empty; one has an open basalt sarcophagus in it; another contains a granite sarcophagus (see Figure 3). The passage spreads out for another ten meters and finally moves 90 degrees around a corner, leading into a room about nine meters square.

This room is filled about three-quarters of the way up the walls with crystal-clear groundwater that covers another sarcophagus. The lid has been pushed slightly to one side and secured with two wooden beams. Hawass claims that this is a symbolic tomb for the god Osiris and that the remains of a skeleton were found in the sarcophagus. This, he says, shows that the structure was never created for a royal burial.

Figure 3. One floor of the Osiris-lake cave on the Giza plateau.

Twenty-two years after my conversation with Adel in the Mena House Hotel, my associate Ramon Zürcher and I crawled into the same shaft, down to the groundwater. I briefly reported about it in 2012.[22] At the time, I knew about Zahi Hawass's claims, but seeing it all for myself, I could only tear my hair out thinking of what he had said. As Adel said: "It drives you crazy." Ordinary people are expected to believe the most unspeakable nonsense!

The underground structure did, in fact, consist of shafts and several chambers. But Hawass had claimed that it had served as a "symbolic grave" for the god Osiris, and that nothing was found apart from the remains of a skeleton. Good heavens! In a sarcophagus that is thousands of years old, you either find nothing at all—because nothing was ever put into it or because grave robbers have stolen everything—or you find a mummy with linens and all the trimmings. Even assuming that someone had actually put a body in the sarcophagus millennia ago, it would never have turned into a skeleton. Skeletons are the result of worms, beetles, and ants nibbling on a body in damp soil. A sarcophagus, on the other hand, is sealed airtight. No critters dine there.

Moreover, since Hawass claimed to have found ceramics from the Sixth Dynasty, the site should have been at least 4,000 years old. At that time, however, there were no grave robbers. They only appeared later. In fact, during the Sixth Dynasty, there would have been no reason to create a pseudo-tomb. Just picture a group of men with primitive stone tools hammering out very deep shafts, scraping out rooms, and using unknown methods to keep the groundwater away—which, even then, flowed continuously. And to top it all off, picture them moving several sarcophagi into the deep structure through narrow shafts, at least one of which was smaller than the stone containers themselves. Why would anyone go to all that trouble for a pseudo-grave?

Zahi Hawass located several rooms deep down in the passages under the Chephren pyramid, one of them measuring 13.25 meters in length, 6.8 meters in width, and 3.5 meters in height. Well, that's more than a room; that's a small hall! He was also looking for hidden entrances, so he had the groundwater pumped out and sent a boy down into a shaft that led from the northwest corner of the lowest room. He tied a rope to the boy's left ankle so that he could be pulled out in an emergency. The boy crawled about five meters into the shaft, but then it became too narrow. To this day, it remains a mystery how the original tunnel builders hollowed out the rock to form the hall when not even a small boy could get through the narrow shaft.

In November 2008, TV producer Richard Reisz sent an endoscope-equipped camera into the same tunnel. After ten meters, rocks prevented any further progress. In December of the same year, a small robot rattled through the same shaft. It discovered a fork about 10.5 meters in, but the way forward from there was blocked. According to Zahi Hawass, the tunnel should be at least twenty-one meters long. And yet the shafts were certainly made to lead somewhere. Tunnels always lead from one point to another. So what was the purpose of these shafts and where were they leading if, in fact, the structure was just a pseudo-grave for the god Osiris?

Throughout our long evening together at the Mena House bar, I kept a small dictation machine running—with Adel's consent, of course. Whenever he didn't want something recorded, I simply turned it off. This was the case when I asked him if he had also crawled into secret rooms or libraries. Here is what he told me, reconstructed from memory and from my notes.

"We know of rooms that are partially flooded with groundwater," Adel said. "Objects are stacked in them, but we have no idea of what they are. They don't look like books. At least not according to what we mean by books. They don't appear to be parchment or papyrus, let alone stone or metal."

"Do you have photos?" I asked.

"No," he replied. "But I can describe what I saw. There are hundreds of holes in the walls, just like those used for mummified birds or monkeys. In each hole is a canopic jar (a ceramic vessel) and in the jars is something that resembles a kind of tube about ten centimeters long. It is hard on the inside and yet made of neither metal or stone; on the outside, there is something elastic, like a rubber cover."

I was wide awake now and wanted to learn more. But Adel literally begged me to end the conversation. He didn't want to talk about it anymore. Then he gulped down two glasses of wine and retired for the night. The next morning at breakfast, however, we returned to our conversation.

MODERN MEASURES

"I've been thinking about these ancient libraries for a long time," Adel began. "The ancients hid tens or even hundreds of thousands of their writings—secured against floods, you said. So some of these hiding places should still exist."

Between several sips of tea, I replied: "We don't do things much differently today. It's just that very few people know about it. In Baden Württemberg, one of the German federal states bordering on Switzerland, there is a small town called Oberried, located about fifteen kilometers east of the city of Freiburg, in the Breisgau district.

Not far from Oberried, there is a tunnel hidden under granite and gneiss known as the Barbarastollen (Barbara tunnel). Except for the locals, nobody has any idea what is being collected down there."

This tunnel is, in fact, the central storage repository of the Federal Republic of Germany. The area is a no-fly zone, and not even German military vehicles are allowed to use the road that leads to the Barbarastollen. Moreover, no airport or radio station is allowed nearby.

The tunnel is around 700 meters long and lined with thick concrete to render it capable of withstanding a nuclear blast. In 1954, when the Hague Convention was signed in the Netherlands by over a hundred countries, special protective rights were granted to the Barbarastollen and fifteen other similar facilities worldwide. In the event of a war, all agreed that these places were not to be targeted.

This tunnel currently contains around 1,500 hermetically sealed barrels with rubber rings around the outside, each weighing 122 kilograms. They contain thousands of microfilms. The whole tunnel serves only one purpose: to preserve the history of the country for generations to come. There, the children of the future will find everything from the coronation certificate of Otto the Great in 936, to the text of the Peace of Westphalia, to the blueprints for the Cologne cathedral. "The tunnel," as Boris Pofalla writes in the *Welt am Sonntag*, "is not a house of treasures, but rather a huge filing cabinet." The Basic

Law (German constitution) alone takes up 3,000 pages, documenting "the entire process leading to the law." Should war come, Pofalla reports, "the entrance would be covered with sand. And twenty years later, nobody would know anything about it."[23]

Adel kept shaking his head. "It is like what Plato said two and a half thousand years ago: We become children again and again, without ever learning about what happened in the past."

"You are right, Adel," I agreed. "And there are fifteen other facilities worldwide like the Barbarastollen. The entire variety of the world's seeds are stored in Spitsbergen in Norway—over a million seed samples, from potatoes and rice to wheat, grass, and various types of corn, to every conceivable flower and crop. The facility, which is under the aegis of the United Nations, is called the Doomsday Seed Vault, or Svalbard Global Seed Vault. Spitsbergen is part of the Arctic Circle; the North Pole is just 1,000 kilometers away. The site is designed in such a way that it will remain sealed despite climate change and rising water levels."

"But what's the use of all that if people in the future don't know about it?" Adel asked, pouring more sugar into his already very sweet tea. "What is the point when former dry areas are under water? When deserts become icebergs and vice versa? Why bother if our descendants can't read the microfilms? And if we can create these repositories, surely some of our forefathers must have done the same. Some of their archives must still exist somewhere."

"Societies throughout time and across cultures have created repositories like these," I replied. "The Mormon Church has a gigantic archive of billions of data points in the Granite Mountain Record Vault near Salt Lake City. The Church of Scientology is no different. One hundred and forty tons of books are stored in the Trementia Base in California. In fact, there are probably more than fifty such systems worldwide. Believe me, I know what I'm talking about.[24]

"It always amazes me," I continued, "how little people know about the global library system. My home country, Switzerland, is small, but our libraries—like the Central Library in Zurich or the Swiss National Library in Bern—are huge. Millions of books are stored there. Or the German National Library, with locations in both Leipzig and Frankfurt, which has no fewer than thirty-three million "media units," as they are called today. Have you ever heard of the Library of Congress in Washington? It manages a whopping 130 million works. Now add the holdings of other libraries from other nations—France, Spain, Britain, Italy, Russia, Greece, and Asian countries—and you will quickly find that there are billions of books stored today worldwide."

Adel stared at me for a few minutes and tapped the table so nervously that the toast crumbs started to dance.

"Billions of books, and they are distributed all over the world," he pondered. "The nations of the world, together with the UN, spend an unimaginably large amount of money on these libraries. And yet it is all for nothing, as the past seems to show us. The old cultures also kept huge libraries. But where are they today?"

I gently pressed the back of Adel's hand onto the table top to calm him. "Despite the destruction that has occurred over the millennia, some of these libraries *must* still exist today. After all, the ancients knew about the coming flood. They knew the story of the wars and looting, so they ended up hiding their treasures. Today, we refer to our collections as 'nuclear-bomb-proof.' But they faced a different set of challenges."

Having heard some of our discussion from the next table, Sahir, another tour guide, joined us and asked if he could listen in on our conversation. Sahir seemed a little nervous and kept blinking his eyes. And he didn't want to admit that our ancestors' libraries had either been destroyed or had even disappeared. For me the topic was old news, as I had dealt with it several times in my books.[25] As we talked, however, more and more curious tourists joined us. Finally, we pushed some tables together and the breakfast room became a seminar room.

PREDATIONS OF MAN

"I don't have to tell you about the destruction caused by various natural disasters," I began. "These things are known. But what nature couldn't accomplish, the beast called 'man' managed to do." I went on to tell the sad tale.

Pharaoh Ramses III (1221–1156 BC) had a huge library compiled during his reign. None of it exists anymore, however. It was destroyed by human folly, not natural disasters. Even the educated Roman general Julius Caesar (100–44 BC) had libraries destroyed during his campaigns. When he let his troops rage in the port of Alexandria in 47 BC, the famous library there went up in flames, destroying an estimated 700,000 books. Then the seductive Cleopatra received 200,000 volumes from the library in Pergamon—both originals and copies. These books were intended to form the basis of a new Alexandrian library. But the Roman emperor Diocletian (c. 240–313 AD) destroyed them all. A third attempt to bring the Alexandrian library to new splendor by copying and compiling ancient texts failed when Theodosius I (347–395 AD) had the library burned down again. And in 562 AD, the Caliph of Damascus, Umar ibn al-Chattab (579–644 AD), came up with the perverse idea of heating all the city's baths by burning texts from the library. After about six months, there were no more books left. Even the much praised Alexander the Great (356–323 BC) did not act more sensibly. We owe the destruction of the *Avesta,* the original religious texts of the Parsis, to him."

Some of my audience were becoming restless, but some commented that there had also been libraries in Ethiopia, China, and in distant Central America.

"Yes, true!" I acknowledged. "And in China, it was the emperor Qin Shi Huang Di (259–210 BC) who burned down all the libraries of his enemies. In Ethiopia, Italian soldiers, spurred on by fanatical Christian priests, set fire to the Royal Libraries of Addis Ababa. Even in far-away India, the huge library of Nalanda University (today in the state of Bihar) was razed to the ground by the Turkish conqueror Muhammad bin Bakhti-yar Khalji (c. 1160–1206 AD)."

"Good God!" one of the tourists exclaimed. "You sound as if they were all fools back then. Surely there must have been some peaceful people on Earth—culturally educated people who disapproved of the destruction and prevented some of it."

"There were," I agreed. "But these sophisticated minds were largely unsuccessful." There was silence in the group. One listener, who introduced himself as a high-school teacher from Clermont-Ferrand, France, wanted to know if any books had been destroyed in South and Central America. "I ask because there were no connections to the distant Americas at that time," he said. "The European generals did not even know the American continents existed."

"As far as South America is concerned," I replied, trying not to be a lecturer or appear opinionated, "we don't know of any documents. The Inca used cords as a memory aid—the so-called *quipus*. And no writings are known of the primeval forest peoples of the Amazon. But the situation in Central America is quite different. There were thousands and thousands of Mayan manuscripts. And all but a few were intentionally burned." I went on to explain.

On July 12, 1562, 5,000 so-called idols, 13 altars, 197 cult vessels, and hundreds of illustrated Mayan manuscripts were piled up in front of the Church of San Miguel in Mani and lit on fire by soldiers on the orders of Bishop Diego de Landa (1524–1579). The flames devoured irreplaceable documents of a great culture. De Landa describes the event thus:

> *We found a large number of books with drawings. But since they contained only lies and the work of the devil, we burned them all, which deeply aggrieved the Maya and caused them great sorrow.* [26]

In the months and years that followed, Christian missionaries blindly destroyed all the writings they could find. Described by Bishop de Landa as "devil's work," all traces of the ancient Mayan religion were erased. In his later justification, *Relación de Las Cosas de Yucatán* (English title: *Report from Yucatán*), de Landa noted: "The most important thing that the chiefs carried into their tribal areas was their scientific books," while his compatriot José de Acosta (1539–1600) reported: "In Yucatán, there existed bound and folded books in which the trained Indians kept their knowledge of the planets, the things of nature, and their ancient traditions." [27]

"It seems to be in the nature of man to destroy everything of which he has no knowledge," I lamented, "everything that seems strange to him or even just disturbs him, especially when it comes to religious texts, regardless of whether in Ancient Egypt, in India, in Europe, or in distant Central America."

At that, the audience went silent. Some walked out slowly, as if feeling guilty. Only the teacher from Clermont-Ferrand wanted to know where I had acquired my knowledge. I told him that I had collected a lot of material on the subject because I planned to write a book about the Maya. Finally, the man introduced himself as Jean-Claude Du-Bois. Before he became a teacher, he said, he had studied Catholic theology for five years. Then love entered his life and he changed his career path. He wanted to know if I was familiar with the Church's shredding of books in Europe, and then went on to explain.

"In 1242," Jean-Claude told us, "at the behest of Pope Gregory IX (1227–1241), a full twenty-four wagonloads of Jewish books were burned. Although Gregory IX was no longer in office in 1242, the destruction of the books was ordered as the result of a judicial process he had initiated. The Jewish writings had been gathered from across France. In Paris, the fires burned for two days. It was called 'the Talmud burning.' Popes Innocent IV (1243–1254), Clemens IV (1256–1268), John XXII (1316–1334), and Paul IV (1555–1559) all issued similar orders for the destruction of books. And in 1559, the *Index Librorum Prohibitorum*, the list of prohibited books, went into effect."

"I know," I interrupted. "I myself spent six years in a Jesuit Catholic boarding school. We were still taught that anyone who read a work from this list of prohibitions would automatically be excommunicated—excluded from the Church and its sacraments. According to this prohibition," I laughed, "I should have been excluded from the Church long ago, even though I pay a tithe every year. In practice, however, I guess I have never lost my deep belief in what is commonly called 'dear God' and I'm still one of those who pray."

Jean-Claude stared at me as if I had lost my mind. Adel, who sat quietly, sipping tea and nodding from time to time, confirmed that he too was a believer in God, even if he did not sing every surah of the Koran.

When Jean-Claude and his group left to visit the Egyptian antiquities, Adel and I remained alone. After a few moments of comfortable silence, I told him there was something else no scholar was talking about. Encouraged by his eagerness to continue our discussion, I asked him if he was aware of another book that dealt with the prophecies of Enoch—called *The Legends of the Jews Volume 1: From Primeval Times*.[28] This work was published in Frankfurt in 1913, I told him, written by a Jewish rabbi named Micha Josef Berdyczewski, later known as Bin Gorion (1865–1921). The man was a scholar who was familiar with all of the ancient Jewish literature—the Torah as well as the Talmud.

"Never heard of it," growled Adel. So I went on to enlighten him.

THE SAPPHIRE TEXT

"Jewish scholars believe that God not only gave Moses the Ten Commandments," I explained, "but also provided spoken instruction to him. These conversations between Moses and his god were written down, and some of them are in the Talmud."

Adel, who had grown up in the Muslim faith, was unfamiliar with the Talmud, but he listened to me politely.

"In the Talmud," I went on, "you can also read that the text originally came from heaven. But not—and this is where it gets interesting—in the form of a book made of parchment, papyrus, or palm leaves. The text appears inscribed on a sapphire stone."

Responding to a questioning look from Adel, I continued.

"Millennia ago, people knew books and carvings on stone, slate, rock, and clay, and only later on papyrus and parchment. But no one could even imagine a book written on a 'sapphire stone.' The thought of it was completely unthinkable at the time. You couldn't even dream of something like that. But it's different today. In the age of computers and lasers, complete lexicons are stored on microchips. Gigantic amounts of data are also stored on crystals and sapphires."

"And who was supposed to be able to read this book on a sapphire stone?" Adel asked. When I replied that Adam was, he looked at me askance and, for the first time in our conversation, I sensed a note of mockery in his voice. "But Adam was our progenitor; he certainly couldn't read."

"Adam received instruction from an angel named Raziel," I told him. "This is not found in the Talmud, but in an ancient work entitled *The Life of Adam and Eve.*[29] There you also learn that Adam received other instruction as well. Before having any contact with the text inscribed on the sapphire stone, he had to wash himself thoroughly. He was never allowed to approach the stone without care and eventually learned to 'talk' with the strange object—that is, to have a dialog with it. From this stone, Adam also learned everything about astronomy and the earthly calendar. He passed this knowledge on to his son, Seth."

With a napkin, Adel nervously wiped the toast crumbs from the table. Finally, he shook his head and said he didn't believe a word of this.

"That's not what's important," I told him, smiling a little forgivingly. "The important thing is that someone said millennia ago that there was once a book inscribed on a sapphire stone. That doesn't fit at all with any ideas from that time. We talk all the time about libraries that were destroyed, about works on papyrus, parchment, palm leaves, foils, and so on. But most of these works have disappeared, consumed by fire and water or deliberately destroyed by people. But what if other messages from ancient times survived because they were stored more securely on precious stones that could survive the ravages of time and the predations of humans?"

We were both silent for a moment and stared at each other. A fan spun slowly above our heads, stirring the air around us. As Adel ordered his umpteenth tea, he continued to shake his head.

"Books inscribed on precious stones? It's all crazy!" he finally said, stretching his hands out defensively. But after some thought, and carefully articulating every word, he pointed slowly to the floor and said: "I saw a sculpture of the goddess Hathor carved into the wall in addition to the strange, tubular objects I described before. Between her eyes, in the middle of her forehead, was something like a precious stone. I clearly remember the indescribable awe I felt that prevented me from prying out the stone. Even I," he said, getting up and stomping his foot, "who am not superstitious, didn't dare climb the wall and touch the stone."

"Did you say Hathor?" I almost whispered. "Wasn't she the goddess of art and science? Adel, you must take me down there! I have to see it with my own eyes!"

"That's impossible," he said very slowly. Then, as he went on, I detected a note of sarcasm in his voice. "But sometimes miracles happen—they just take a little longer."

I told Adel that what he had described sounded like what is sometimes called the Third Eye, recognized today as the pineal gland. Philosopher and mathematician René Descartes (1596–1650) even located the ancestral seat of the soul in the pineal gland. But the tradition of the Third Eye can also be found in several Indian gods, especially Shiva, an important member of the Hindu pantheon. Statues of Shiva show a Third Eye in the middle of the forehead. And in a similar Egyptian tradition, the "eye of Horus" sees all. Nothing escapes this eye. It keeps watch over all.

"I myself wonder if Horus, the son of Osiris and Isis, was actually a satellite that monitored Earth," I speculated, "serving as a Third Eye that knows everything and stores all knowledge."

With that, Adel and I finished our tea and left the hotel, each thinking deeply on what we had discussed.

THE DESTRUCTION CONTINUES

I am writing this book thirty-four years after the discussions Adel and I had at the Mena House Hotel. Yet even today, the destruction of libraries continues unabated. Year after year, so-called warriors of the Islamic state destroy cultural artifacts of all kinds. Anything that doesn't originate from their own tradition is being destroyed. The Mosul Museum, 400 kilometers north of Baghdad—destroyed, along with 100,000 books and ancient writings. The ancient Assyrian city of Nimrud, thirty kilometers south of Mosul in northern Iraq—destroyed, along with many treasures that had not yet been cataloged and are therefore lost forever. The Syrian desert city of Palmyra, the former Tadmor, home to many temples and libraries—destroyed several times over. Christian storm troopers raged through the city in the fourth and fifth centuries, followed by Islamic extremists in the 21st century. In Timbuktu (Mali in Africa), the rebel group Ansar Dine destroyed fourteen mausoleums, including their libraries.

Timbuktu had for centuries been an important cultural center of the Islamic world. But no more.

And today, these repositories are being annihilated through technology. A short circuit at the National Museum of Brazil in Rio de Janeiro resulted in a fire that destroyed that important collection in September 2018. The museum had been founded in 1818 by King John VI of Portugal (1767–1826), and was home to the richest anthropological library in Brazil. Twenty million exhibits were lost forever. Indeed, it seems as if we humans are incapable of preserving our history and carrying our ancestral legacy into the future. Are we, as Plato stated, doomed to start all over again like children?

Half an hour later, Adel and I were sitting in a smelly Volkswagen with rusted-out door hinges and a wobbly rear wheel. Adel, who was trained as a taxi driver, navigated the chaotic streets of Cairo skillfully. As he stopped to yield to traffic, he looked over at me and said: "You don't know that, when I was sixteen, I was trapped in the labyrinths under the Saqqara pyramid for several days. At the time, many newspapers wrote about the miracle of how I escaped alive. I'll tell you the story another time."

Between the never-ending din of the Cairo streets, the constant stop-and-go of traffic, and the ranting of other drivers, I replied: "A phenomenal labyrinth must exist somewhere in Egypt. Many ancient historians have reported about it. Do you know anything about it?"

"Just vaguely," he shouted over at me. "I am familiar with the literature on it, and I'm pretty well informed about the labyrinths."

And that began one of the most astonishing conversations Adel and I would ever have.

CHAPTER 3

Vanished Labyrinths

A LABYRINTH IS A MAZE, a system of paths or corridors through which no one can find their way. Labyrinths teem with dead ends. They are mind-boggling systems engineered to demoralize, frighten, and defeat anyone who tries to find the exit. They can also serve as effective prisons.

Several ancient writers have reported on labyrinths over the centuries. For instance, on the Mediterranean island of Crete, there is said to have been a labyrinth in which a monster called the Minotaur was imprisoned. This creature is described as a hybrid being—a human body with a bull's head. But how did such a monster ever get imprisoned on Crete?

THE CRETAN LABYRINTH

The story told by ancient writers is bursting with contra-dictions and inconsistencies. It all started with the power-ful god the Greeks called Zeus. The Romans called him Jupiter and, in various Germanic groups, he is also known as Thor, Odin, or Wotan. According to Greek mythology, twelve Titans—male and female giants with immense power—once came from the starry sky (called Uranos). The Titans fathered children, including the sun god, Helios, and the moon goddess, Selene. Chronos, one of these Titans, impregnated his own sister, thus fathering Zeus. Zeus' siblings were Poseidon, god of the seas, and Hades, god of the underworld. Between them, the three ruled over the heavens, the oceans, and the lower regions.

Zeus came to be known by a number of names—God of Thunder, Lightning Thrower, Wise One, and even Transformer, because he could appear as any living being and in various disguises. He appeared to Leda as a swan, to Europa as a bull, to Callisto as a young Apollo, and to Danaë as a shower of gold. But he was also attracted to good-looking adolescent males, and he fell in love with Prince Ganymede, whom he immediately kidnapped and took to Olympus.

With his wife, Europa, Zeus fathered Minos, who in turn asked his uncle, Poseidon, to grant him a miracle and make him king of Crete. In return, Minos promised to sacrifice to Poseidon everything that emerged from the sea. Upon hearing this, Poseidon brought forth from his domain a magnificent white bull with extraordinary properties and gave it to Minos as a gift. But Minos, cunning as he was, wanted to keep the unique animal and hid it among his herd. To satisfy Poseidon, he sacrificed an ordinary bull instead.

And that's where the trouble started. Poseidon discovered the betrayal and hypnotized Pasiphaë, Minos's wife, causing her to fall madly in love with the bull. The love-stricken Pasiphaë approached Daedalus, a famous artisan and engineer from Athens, to help her have sex with the beautiful bull. Daedalus built a wooden frame and covered it with a cowhide. Then the smitten Pasiphaë lay in the frame in such a way that the bull's penis could penetrate her vagina. The bull mated with Pasiphaë and the fruit of this union was the Minotaur, a man with a bull's head. She called the monster Asterios. Quickly recognizing that the Minotaur was easily enraged and prone to destroy buildings and even kill people, she asked Daedalus for help controlling and confining the beast. Daedalus built a confusing maze from which the Minotaur could never escape—the infamous labyrinth of Crete.

The human-animal monster had hideous desires. It demanded that seven children and seven young virgins be sacrificed to it every nine years. Theseus, a son of the King of Athens, wanted to end this gruesome ritual. He bravely snuck into the group of sacrificial victims during the third sacrifice with the intention of killing the Minotaur. But before the sacrifice took place, he fell in love with Ariadne, a daughter of King Minos. Ariadne asked Daedalus for advice on how her lover could find his way out of the impenetrable labyrinth after killing the Minotaur. Daedalus, who had a solution for every problem, showed the king's daughter the exit of the labyrinth, which lay close to its entrance, and handed her a ball of wool—the now famous "Ariadne's thread." He told Ariadne to have Theseus tie this thread to his person at the entrance and unroll the ball of wool behind him as he went.

Theseus killed the Minotaur with a sword, then followed "Ariadne's thread" to the labyrinth's exit. The king, learning of Daedalus' role in this plot, had him and his son, Icarus, thrown into prison. But Minos underestimated the shrewdness of this engineer. Daedalus constructed two belts made of light wood, feathers, and resin, and, using them as wings to cleverly trap the power of the wind, escaped to freedom with his son. They soared over the island of Crete and out over the Mediterranean Sea.

Before they took off, Daedalus had made it clear to his son that, wherever possible, he should fly under the clouds to avoid the heat of the sun lest it melt the resin holding their wings together. Icarus, however, did not take his father's warning seriously and flew above the clouds. The heat of the sun melted the resin with which his wings were attached, the wings loosened, and Icarus fell. Since then, this area of the Mediterranean has been called the Icarian Sea, and the island where the body of Icarus washed ashore is called Icaria.

Daedalus, however, escaped to Sicily, where he was enthusiastically received by King Cocalus. After all, every ruler wants to have technical superiority over others and Daedalus had proven his worth as an engineer. King Minos, however, was furious. His fleet put to sea to look for Daedalus, and he sent out envoys to enquire about a strange man who may have fallen from the sky. As an incentive, Minos offered a reward for solving a riddle that he assumed only the clever Daedalus could solve: How do you pull a thread through a spiraled snail shell? Taking up the challenge, Daedalus proceeded to solve the riddle. He drilled the snail's casing, fastened a thin thread to an ant, and let the animal crawl through the hole. He placed a few drops of honey at the entrance of the shell and the ant, drawn by the sweetness, navigated the shell, pulling the thread behind it.

When Minos heard of the solution, he realized immediately that only Daedalus could have come up with it and demanded that the Sicilian king deliver him up. But Cocalus no longer wanted to give up his valuable technician. So, feigning hospitality, he invited Minos to his palace. When Minos arrived, he offered him a bath after his travels. Minos is said to have been scalded to death with hot water by pretty girls.

Many ancient historians have reported on the legend of the Cretan labyrinth and Daedalus—Homer and Hesiod, Thucydides, Pindar, Plutarch, Pliny the Elder, Diodorus of Sicily, and of course the "father of history," the Greek philosopher Herodotus. They may report different versions and include different story elements, but the main story remains the same. The Greek writer Flavius Philostratos (c. 165/170–244/249 AD) wrote that a labyrinth in Knossos, the residence of King Minos, was once known to have enclosed the Minotaur. But Plutarch (45–125 AD), the eloquent ancient philosopher, noted:

> *Not long afterward, the emissaries came from Crete for the third time to pick up the toll . . . seven children and seven virgins . . . were killed by the Minotaur in the labyrinth or wandered around in it, could not find the exit, and had died . . . But the Cretans claim that the labyrinth was nothing more than a prison from which prisoners simply couldn't escape.*[1]

So which is correct? Was the labyrinth a maze for the Minotaur or just a prison for people?

THE PALACE AT KNOSSOS

Several modern researchers have tried to locate the labyrinth in Crete but have found nothing except caves. So where are the remains of this ancient labyrinth? In 1958, French archaeologist Paul Faure (1916–2007) announced that he had been there. But he was wrong. What he had found turned out to be merely a cave. Previously, Joseph Pitton de Tournefort (1656–1708), who was a member of the French Academy of Sciences, claimed to have found "the labyrinth at Gortyn" on Crete:

> *This famous place is an underground passage, like an alley,*
> *laid out in a hundred bends that were created randomly and*
> *without the slightest order, inside a hill at the foot of Mount*
> *Ida, 3 miles from the ruins of Gortyn.*[2]

But de Tournefort's find also turned out to be a hoax. Gortyn was the capital of Crete in Roman times and its origins are said to go back as far as 6,000 years before Christ. This would actually fit with the legend of Minotaur. But archaeologists have shown that the material for the construction of Gortyn came from a quarry located north of the village of Kastelli near the Cretan city of Mires. These hills are riddled with caves, some of which have clearly been dredged. In fact, one of these caves was used by the Nazis as an ammunition depot during World War II. Although these caves are still presented to tourists as the original labyrinth, none of this is true.

The person most familiar with all labyrinths was undoubtedly the German lawyer and art historian Hermann Kern (1941–1985). In his brilliant work *Labyrinths*, he discusses all conceivable possible locations for the Cretan labyrinth and comes to the conclusion that none of the ancient writers had ever visited the real labyrinth— if it existed at all—nor had any contemporary researcher.[3]

English archeologist Arthur Evans (1851–1941) came to Crete in 1894 and, just like German archeologist Heinrich Schliemann (1822–1890) before him, he believed in the accuracy of the ancient accounts. He relied on the ancient philosopher Homer, the author of the *Iliad* and the story about its hero, Odysseus. Homer, who is believed to have written sometime between 800 and 1200 BC, reported in great detail on Crete—on its legends, on the labyrinth, and on the royal palace of Knossos, which was the residence of King Minos at the time during which the labyrinth and the Minotaur are said to have existed.

Evans, who became director of the Ashmolean Museum in Oxford, raised money and gained sponsors enough so that he could excavate in Crete. On March 23, 1900, he landed on Crete with thirty men. Layer by layer, the men tore open the ground, searching for the palace of King Minos and hoping to find the famed labyrinth. They eventually proved that a cult that worshipped the bull had, indeed, been active on Crete. Motifs to that effect appeared on murals and ceramics showing bulls and bull horns (see Figure 4). But nowhere could they find the entrance to a labyrinth or to the workshop of Daedalus. Nor did they find any bones of the Minotaur monster. The one thing Evans was able to prove was that Homer's descriptions were quite correct. But it was the dating of the finds that caused the most confusion.

Excavations showed clearly that the palace of King Minos had been destroyed and rebuilt several times, and the dimensions of even the oldest complex, which was dated from around 5000 BC, were approximately the same size as the newest. But that didn't deter Evans. He was convinced that an entrance to the labyrinth had to be located somewhere underground. After continued excavation, researchers uncovered scattered megalithic blocks dating from the Stone Age, around 8000 BC, but no trace of a labyrinth.

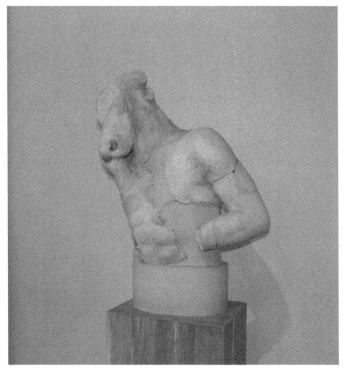

Figure 4. Statue of the Minotaurus in the Cretan archaeological museum in Heraklion.

The walls of the palace at Knossos turned out to be an interlaced complex of inner courtyards, halls, and smaller chambers (see Figure 5). Over a thousand rooms were uncovered (see color insert).

Then tub-shaped vessels with drainage holes were found, but no means for drainage to the outside. A large number of stairs, often only ten meters in height, led to a rooftop terrace probably large enough to accommodate all the palace residents. Evans and his group also came across several storage rooms filled with two-meter-tall

Figure 5. Model of the Minoan palace in the Cretan archaeological museum in Heraklion.

clay pots (see Figures 6, 7, and 8). What purpose did they serve? In his book *Wohin der Stier Europa trug (Where the Bull Carried Europa)*, German geologist Hans Georg Wunderlich (1928–1974) speculates:

> *Even with normal storage jars, one wonders how they were actually emptied and cleaned from time to time, since even with very long trowels you can hardly reach the bottom, even if you use a stool. The giant pithoi [clay pots] pose an insoluble problem in this regard: they can't even be tilted.*
>
> *Storage vessels the size of these giant pithoi had to be brought in, stood up and then walled in before the surrounding walls were erected, without the possibility of later replacing them with other vessels. Filling and emptying was probably only possible with the help of hoses, based on the principle of connected tubes. But how impractical to install such vessels in a place that is difficult to access! You turn away confused.*[4]

New calculations show that a single one of these monstrous jugs held an average of 586 liters. "The total number of all the containers housed in the west wing of the Palace of Knossos alone amounted to 420, which corresponded to a storage capacity of 226,000 liters," Ralf Sonnenberg notes.[5] But such "oil containers," often called cisterns by archaeologists, were kept, not only in the western part of the palace, but in all larger buildings. The storage capacity was gigantic. What were they used for? Sir Arthur Evans suggests that the Minoans were preparing for emergencies.

Figures 6 and 7. Oil tanks in the ruins of the Minoan Palace in Knossos.

Figure 8. Oil tanks with mixed creatures in the Cretan archaeological museum in Heraklion.

But that can't be right. Knossos did not fear invasion and was in no danger. The whole island of Crete was unpaved, and there were no walls around it. Crete was not afraid of enemies, which is why the palace at Knossos was not surrounded by a wall. The ruler was the son of a god with special skills, and a robot was constantly circling the island.

I beg your pardon?

ROBOTS AND FLYING MACHINES

Hephaistos, a son of Zeus, is said to have constructed an indestructible guardian named Talos, whom Zeus personally sent to Crete to protect the island. Talos possessed an invulnerable, metallic body. In ancient literature, he was described as a "bronze giant"[6] or as a being "that was coated with ore all over."[7] Apollonius of Rhodes, who lived sometime during the fourth century BC and reported extensively on the odyssey of the ship Argo and its crew, the Argonauts, wrote that Talos circled around the island of Crete three times a year.[8] Other authors of the time speak of "three times a day."

Talos had magical eyes that he aimed at any ship that approached the island of Crete without permission. Then he shot at unwelcome vessels from a great distance. He had the ability to radiate heat, pull boats to him, and burn them up. Although unassailable, Talos had a weak spot—a tendon in his ankle that was covered with tanned skin, hiding a metal nail or screw. If this tanned skin was compromised or lost, colorless blood gushed out of the opening and Talos lost his ability to move.

The *Argonautica* describes how Jason, the captain of the Argo, approached the island of Crete. The robot Talos promptly spotted the ship and fired at it. But Jason's wife knew a spell that could paralyze Talos. She irritated the robot's eyes in such a way that he "saw dream images" and slammed into a rock. Suddenly, blood "flowed like liquid lead" from a wound on his ankle.

> *Although he was metallic, he succumbed to the magic . . .*
> *he hit a pointed stone, a juice flows out like molten lead. He*
> *could no longer stand upright and tipped over like a spruce*
> *that falls on the top of a mountain . . . so he got up again*

and stood on his mighty feet. But not for a long time, soon he
fell on the ground with a loud sound.[9]

Talos staggered back and forth, finally losing his balance and falling into the sea with a gruesome roar. The remains of this automatic, radar-eyed weapon are probably still there today.

Evans, failing to find the labyrinth, finally assumed that the word "labyrinth" referred to the palace of Minos itself, which was interlaced with courtyards and rooms. But this view does not match the descriptions of the labyrinth at all. King Minos's residence may be confusing, but it is in no way like a labyrinth. The palace does not correspond to any description of the maze purportedly built by Daedalus, and no room was located anywhere that would have fit the story of the Minotaur monster. Did this Minotaur really exist? And what purpose did the incredible storage capacity of the oil jars described above serve?

Well, let's speculate a little.

From *Kebra Nagast*, the millennia-old epic account of the kings of Ethiopia, we know that King Solomon had several flying machines with which he visited his beloved, the queen of Saba.[10] These flying machines were not extraterrestrial vehicles, but zeppelin-like hot-air balloons, powered and controled by modest steam engines. But you need fire and water to produce steam. And the easiest way to make portable fire is by burning oil in a container. This heats the water to the boiling point, and the steam generated could ultimately drive a primitive propeller.

Now, the Roman historian Pliny the Elder tells us, in the sixth book of his *Natural History*, that a branch of the

Minoans lived far from Crete, in distant Yemen.[11] So it is possible that the giant clay jugs in the palace at Knossos could have been a fuel depot intended to power balloons of this kind. And the numerous stairs in the chamber that led to the large flat roof also make sense in this context. If such a hot-air balloon approached, people could run onto the flat roof to receive and tether it. Such arrivals and departures would have been treated as spectacles, attracting all the residents of the palace.

HYBRID CREATURES

And what about the Minotaur itself—a hybrid being with a bull's body and a human head? All just pure imagination and lies? We know today that hybrid beings are biologically impossible. Humans and animals have different numbers and sets of chromosomes that simply are not compatible. All humans have what is called the "simple chromosome set," which consists of twenty-three pairs of chromosomes. Animals have different sets of chromosomes. If a man were so perverse as to get involved with a female ape, their offspring would not be a human/ape hybrid. It is rumored that the Russian tsarina Catherine II (1729–1796) mated with her gray stallion. But this did not lead to the birth of a centaur—beings that are half human and half horse.

Centaurs existed in Greek mythology, but they were said to have been created by the mating of Ixion, the king of the Lapiths, with a cloud. These beasts were considered carnal beings. At a wedding celebration, several drunken centaurs are said to have attacked the ladies present. But also present were some wise and highly intelligent centaurs. The most famous of these was Cheiron, who was created by the Titan Chronos and was said to have raised several Greek heroes, including Achilles and Asclepios (see Figures 9 and 10). Jason, the captain of the Argo in the history of *Argonautica*, was also brought up by a centaur.

Figures 9 and 10. Centaurs in the Cretan archaeological museum in Heraklion.

So was the story of the Minotaur just imagination and human invention? Were there ever any hybrid beasts? I contend that there probably were such beasts, but that they were created in a different way than ancient people could have imagined. Although the Minotaur of Crete could never have originated from a mating between a bull and Pasiphaë, it could still have existed. But how?

In ancient Egypt, there lived a sacred bull named Apis that was revered by the people—a relative of the Minotaur, so to speak (see Figures 11 and 12). Apis was also known to become enraged, devastate fields, collapse temples, and kill old people and children alike. Herodotus, the Greek historian who lived in Egypt for a few years, wrote:

> *The so-called Apis has the following markings: he is black; he has a triangular, white spot on his forehead, on his back the image of an eagle, tail hairs doubled, and visible under the tongue is the image of a beetle.*[12]

The ancient Egyptians saw the divine bull as a descendant of the cosmos, a creation of the god Ptah. This earliest veneration is evidenced by palettes with star-studded bulls' heads that appeared in Abydos, as well as golden sun disks that were clamped between Apis's horns (see color insert). Abydos itself is fascinating for its megalithic walls built of perfectly fitted stone that date back into the mists of time.

Greek historian Plutarch (c. 50 AD) reports that this divine bull did not come into being naturally, but rather through a ray that fell from the sky. This origin myth appears to be confirmed on a sepulchral stele found by French archeologist Auguste Mariette (1821–1881), founder of the Egyptian Museum, in the underground complex of the Serapeum near Saqqara, where a depiction of an Apis bull is topped by an inscription that reads: You have no father—you are made from heaven.[13]

Figures 11 and 12. Divine Apis bulls with sun disks between their horns.

Whether in Crete, Egypt, Greece, or elsewhere, hybrid beings appear to be associated with the gods and with the starry sky. In the Sumerian *Epic of Gilgamesh,* Gilgamesh, the king of Uruk, is described as a hybrid being: "This is how the great gods Shamash and Adal created Gilgamesh. He was eleven cubits tall . . . two thirds god, one third man."[14] The Sphinx that stands in front of the Great Pyramid is also a hybrid being. The so-called flying genii that appear on Sumerian scroll seals are hybrids as well. And the figures on the black obelisk of the Assyrian King Salamasar II (859–824 BC), which is now in the British Museum in London, clearly depict hybrids. A tall man is chiseled in the stone of the obelisk leading strange animals on a rope or a chain. The small creatures clearly have human heads—one sucks on his thumb, the other shows his long nose—but both beings have the bodies of animals (see Figure 13).

Figure 13. Hybrid creatures on the black obelisk of the Assyrian King Salamazar II in the British Museum in London.

The chain and the rope with which the hybrid creatures are being led indicate that they must have been assumed to have lived.

"Mythical creatures" with lion paws, lion bodies, and human heads are found, not only in Egypt, but in museums around the world. The Asutosh Museum in Calcutta, the Archaeological Museum in Ankara, the Delphi Museum in Greece, and the Metropolitan Museum in New York all boast numerous hermaphroditic creatures and monsters (see Figures 14 and 15). And just because evolution could not have produced these hybrid beings—simply because they couldn't have been created through a sexual act between humans and animals—doesn't mean that they are all just the product of wild imaginations. Historian and ecclesiastical dignitary Eusebius (263–339 AD) confirmed the existence of these hybrid beings very clearly, referring to the Egyptian historian and priest Manetho (third century BC), as well as other sources in the foreword to his *Chronicle*:

> . . . and they [the gods] would have created humans, double-winged; also others with four wings and two faces and one body with two heads . . . and two natures, male and female: other beings with thighs of goats and horns on their heads; still others, horse-footed; and others of horse shape on their back side and human shape on their front side. They also created bulls, with human heads . . . as well as other monsters, varied in nature and different from one another, whose images they keep in the temple of Belos depicted one next to the other.[15]

Figures 14 and 15. Hybrid creatures in the British Museum in London.

Although, millennia ago, humans knew nothing about genetics, today we know that such creatures can, in fact, be created through gene splicing and genetic manipulation.

What remains as an explanation of the mystery of the Cretan labyrinth are the gods to whom Eusebius and all other historians refer. And the gods, I contend, were extraterrestrial astronauts who were looking for various life forms that could live and develop on other planets (hotter, colder, smaller, larger, etc.). These aliens did not have to load hybrid creatures into their spaceships and cart them away, however. Their technology was such that a few grams of DNA would suffice.

THE EGYPTIAN LABYRINTH

The labyrinth of Crete has not yet been found or explained, despite archaeological claims to the contrary. Nor has the enormous labyrinth purported to lie under the Egyptian sands. This labyrinth, which is described as being ten times bigger than that of Crete, still lies undiscovered and untouched somewhere under Egypt's desert floor.

Or so I had thought before Adel revealed to me that either he or members of his grave-robber family may have visited that labyrinth and remained silent about it because of the incredible treasures they found there. In 1989, eight years before Adel's murder, I wrote about the Egyptian labyrinth for the first time in my book *The Eyes of the Sphinx*.[16] Thirty years have passed since then and new information and new sources have come to light.

The incredible story begins in 448 BC, when Herodotus landed in Alexandria. He diligently recorded what the priests, acknowledged as the wise men of the time, entrusted to him. He made clear distinctions between what he heard and what he saw with his own eyes. In the second book of his *Histories* (chapter 148), he describes his personal visit to the labyrinth. I quote it here at length because of its importance to our discussion:

> *They also wanted to leave a common monument [the twelve kings] and therefore built the labyrinth, which is located slightly above Lake Moeris, near the so-called City of Crocodiles. I still saw it; it defies any description. If you put together all the similar wall structures and other structures in Greece, they wouldn't require as much work and money as one labyrinth. The temple of Ephesus and the one on Samos are quite impressive. The pyramids certainly defied any description, and each of them equaled many great works by the Greeks; the labyrinth even surpasses the pyramids. It has twelve covered courtyards whose gates face each other, six in the north, six in the south, all close together. There is a single wall all around them. There are two types of chambers in this building, underground and above ground, a total of 3,000, 1,500 of each type. I walked through the above-ground rooms, observing everything, and I write from my own experience; I was only told about the underground chambers. The Egyptian guards didn't want to show them under any circumstances. They said they contained the coffins of the kings who had built this labyrinth from the beginning and the coffins of the sacred crocodiles. So I can only say what I was told about the lower chambers. The upper ones, which I could see with my own eyes, represent almost superhuman work.*

The exits through the halls and crossways through the court-yards with their bright colors offered wonders upon wonders. You get from the courtyard into the halls, from the halls into the pillared halls, from the halls back into other chambers and from them back into other courtyards. The ceiling is made of stone everywhere, as are the walls; the walls are full of reliefs, each courtyard is surrounded by carefully assembled white marble columns. At the corner at the end of the labyrinth is a forty-fathom high pyramid with huge figures carved into it. An underground passage leads to the inside of the pyramid. This is how huge this labyrinth is. But the so-called Moeris Lake, on whose banks this labyrinth is built, represents an even greater marvel. It has a size of 3,600 stadia, which is sixty schoeni, equating in length the entire sea coast of Egypt. It stretches from north to south and has a maximum depth of fifty clusters. You can clearly see that it is human work and artificially dug. Because, in the middle of the lake, there are two pyramids that protrude 50 fathoms high and extend just as deep into the water. Both pyramids show a colossal picture made of stone, a figure sitting on the throne. So the pyramids are 100 fathoms high. These 100 fathoms mean one stadium of six plethras because one fathom is six feet and four cubits, one foot four hand widths, one cubit six hand widths. The water in the lake isn't water from a well because the area is very dry. It is derived from the Nile through a canal. Six months it flows into the lake, six months it flows out again into the Nile . . . The locals say that the lake has an underground run-off to the Libyan Sirte, and this run-off leads west into the country, along the mountains above Memphis.[17]

The dimensions Herodotus reports here are almost unimaginable. Here are our equivalents to the Greek measurements:

- 1 foot = 30 centimeters

- 1 plethron = 100 feet or 30 meters

- 1 fathom = 1.8 meters

- 1 stadium = 180 meters

- 50 stadia = 9 kilometers

- 2000 stadia = 360 kilometers

Herodotus makes it unmistakably clear that he did *not* see the underground rooms, of which he claims there were 1,500. On the other hand, he emphasizes that he was personally in the rooms above ground, telling us that he "walked through the upper rooms, observing everything, and I write from my own experience."

Herodotus, who knew the size and scope of the pyramids of Giza, concluded that "the labyrinth even surpasses the pyramids." He describes the above-ground rooms as being built of mighty stone slabs: "The ceiling is made of stone everywhere, as are the walls; the walls are full of reliefs." Then he describes a huge artificial lake in the middle of which stand two pyramids, each one hundred fathoms high—fifty fathoms below and fifty fathoms above the water—each adorned with a colossal carving. This makes them higher than the pyramid of Cheops.

Herodotus describes a pyramid that stands next to the labyrinth on the shores of the artificial lake—today, Lake

Moeris. The lake, he says, is "a human marvel with a size of 3,600 stadiums . . . equaling the entire length of the sea coast of Egypt." Converted to today's measurements, this lake would have had a circumference of 648 kilometers. By comparison, the circumference of Lake Constance is 273 kilometers.

Are we to assume that Herodotus was simply over-whelmed by his own imagination? Did he calculate the measurements incorrectly? Do other ancient historians corroborate his description of this labyrinth? After all, Herodotus was not the only prominent visitor to Egypt in ancient times. Almost 400 years after Herodotus, Diodorus of Sicily also stayed in Egypt. In the first book of his universal history *Bibliotheca Historica* (chapter 61), he also reports on the labyrinth:

> *After the death of this king, the Egyptians regained their independence and put a local on the throne, Mendes, whom some also call Marrhos. The latter did not wage any wars, but he built a tomb, the so-called labyrinth, which was not only famous for the grandeur of the structure but also for its inimitable artificiality. Whoever enters it cannot easily find the exit unless he has a very knowledgeable guide at his side. Some also say that Daedalus came to Egypt, admired the art-istry of the work and then built a labyrinth for Minos, King of Crete, similar to that in Egypt, which, according to legend, had imprisoned the so-called Minotaur there. The labyrinth of Crete has now completely disappeared, be it that a ruler tore it down or that time destroyed the work. But the whole of Egypt's structure has remained intact to this day.[18]*

Five chapters later, he tells the same story about the twelve kings and their tomb that Herodotus had told:

> . . . *now twelve of the most powerful among the great conspired together.*
>
> *They held a meeting at Memphis, signed a treaty of mutual friendship and loyalty and declared themselves kings . . . they decided to build one gigantic tomb for all of them . . . It should be something bigger than all the works of their predecessors. They chose a place at the entrance to Lake Moeris in Libya. The tomb was built from the most beautiful stones. From below it was given the shape of a square, each side of which measured a stadium . . . Inside the ring wall a hall was built, each side of which consisted of forty columns. The ceiling was made of stone, with artificially chiseled panels and various colorful paintings. They were memorabilia from the homeland of the individual kings.*[19]

It is not clear whether Diodorus personally visited the labyrinth or whether he copied his description from his predecessor, Herodotus. After all, he claims that the entire Egyptian labyrinth had remained intact up until his writing. And he also locates the labyrinth at Lake Moeris.

Diodorus's colleague, the Greek historian and geographer Strabo of Amaseia (c. 63 BC–23 AD), goes even further. He visited Egypt in the year 25 BC and definitely claims to have seen the labyrinth himself. In book seventeen of his *Geography* (chapter 37), he reports:

> *Due to its size and depth, Lake Moeris is suitable for taking up the overflowing floods during the swelling of the Nile*

*. . . but there are also locks at both estuaries of the canal,
through which the master builder regulated the outflow of
water. There is also the labyrinth, a building that resembles
the pyramids, and next to it the tomb of the king who built
the labyrinth. If you walk about 30–40 stadiums from the
first entrance to the canal, you see an equally four-sided area
with a village and a large palace that consists of as many
palaces as there were nouns in the past.*

*Because there are so many adjoining palace halls, all in a
row and all on one wall . . . In front of the entrances there
are many long, concealed corridors, which have intertwined,
crooked paths, so that without a guide it would be impossible
for any stranger to find the entrance or exit of any palace
hall. It is astonishing, however, that the ceiling of each chamber is made of one slab, and that the widths of the covered
passageways are also clad with slabs of extraordinary size,
that have no wood or any other building material mixed in.
If you climb onto the roof, which is at a significant height,
you will see a stone surface of enormous slabs . . . also the
walls are made of stones of no small size. At the end of this
building, which is more than one stadium wide, is the tomb,
a four-sided pyramid: with sides and height of 400 feet. The
buried one is called Imandes . . . If you pass this building
and go 100 stadia further, you will get to the city of Arsinoe.
It used to be called Crocodile City . . . our innkeeper, one of
the most respected men who showed us the sacred objects there,
went to the lake with us.*[20]

Strabo was an eyewitness. He reported that his innkeeper
brought a hard loaf of bread to the lake and gave it to the

priest so that he could throw it to a crocodile to eat. But the animal was dozing on the lake shore and was too lazy to devour the bread.

Strabo was deeply impressed by the gigantic stone slabs that were used to build the halls. He also compared the size of the labyrinth to the pyramids. But why didn't he mention the 1,500 underground rooms described by Herodotus? There are good reasons for that.

The Romans ruled Egypt during Strabo's visit. Strabo was Greek, but Greece was part of the Roman Empire. Twenty-two years before Strabo's visit, the Roman Emperor Gaius Julius Caesar (100–44 BC) had defeated the Egyptian army and installed his beloved Cleopatra as Queen over Egypt. With this, Egypt became, essentially, a Roman province. It is understandable that the Egyptian priesthood would never dream of delivering their ancient secrets to the hated conquerors. They also feared looting by Caesar and his armies. After all, it was Caesar's soldiers who had raged in Alexandria in 47 BC and set fire to the world-famous library housed there.

Four hundred and twenty-three years before Strabo, Herodotus had not been permitted to visit the underground rooms of the labyrinth. So it is not surprising that Strabo did not hear a word about the underground treasures either. Moreover, nearly half a millennium separated the visits of Strabo and Herodotus. In Herodotus's time, the priests were proud to announce that visitors could see the 1,500 rooms above ground but not the 1,500 that lay below. Over 400 years later, few people even knew about the hidden 1,500 rooms—and those who did were understandably silent for political reasons.

Nevertheless, the historical record clearly shows that the labyrinth existed. The impressive above-ground rooms have been documented and compared in size and scope with the pyramids. And almost 100 years *after* Strabo, people were still talking about this labyrinth, as evidenced by the Roman historian Gaius Plinius Secundus, also called Pliny the Younger (61–113 AD). In the thirty-sixth book of his *Natural History*, Pliny refers to Herodotus but tries hard to correct and supplement his predecessor:

> *Also about the labyrinths, these strangest objects, which were not, as one would like to believe, fictitious works of the human mind.*
>
> *Even now there exists one in the Heracleotic district of Egypt, which is also the oldest one and said to have been built 3,600 years ago by King Petesuchus or Thitoes, while Herodotus says that it was built by twelve kings, the last of whom was Psammetichus. There are various reasons given for its construction . . . there is no doubt that Daedalus used this labyrinth as a model for the one he built, but he only imitated the hundredth part of it . . . So the Daedalus labyrinth was the second one in Egypt, the third was in Lemnos, and the fourth in Italy. All of them were built of polished stones in an arched way, the Egyptian one consists of Parian stones at the entrance, which amazes me, but for the rest its material consists of large blocks of syenite, and even centuries could not destroy it, although the Heracleopolites did as much as*

they could to damage a work they hate . . . [The labyrinth]
also contains the temples of all Egyptian gods, goddesses of
vengeance in forty chapels, several pyramids, each 40 cubits
high, which, at their base, have the size of six fields. Already
tired from walking, you come to those inextricable, confus-
ing corridors. But there are also tall dining rooms upstairs,
and over ninety steps you descend into galleries containing
columns of porphyry, idols, statues of kings and all sorts of
hideous figures. Some of the houses are so long that a ter-
rible thunderous sound is heard inside when the doors are
opened. In most of the labyrinth, you have to walk in the
dark. Outside the wall there are several other large buildings
called wings, and there are also some houses in underground
arched rooms. [21]

Pliny seems to have been there in person, otherwise he
could hardly note that he was "already tired of walking,"
or that "the Egyptian one consists of Parian stones at the
entrance, which amazes me," or that "in most of the labyrinth you have to walk in darkness." He also describes a
"terrible thunder" when opening the doors. He doesn't
only see these things; he hears them. And finally, he states
that some houses are "arched halls underground."

PUZZLING CONTRADICTIONS

After I had told Adel everything I knew about the Egyptian labyrinth and read the texts of ancient historians to
him, I looked at him intently and asked: "Adel, have you
been in this labyrinth?"

Slowly and thoughtfully, he replied that what I had told him completely contradicted what he had known before.

"I don't understand," I replied, giving him a questioning look. "What did you know before?"

"At the university in Vienna, we were taught that the Egyptian labyrinth had long since been discovered by the German archaeologist Karl Richard Lepsius (1810–1884) sometime in the middle of the nineteenth century. The labyrinth he claimed to have found was located in what is now the El Fayoum oasis at the pyramid of Amenemhet III (c. 1844—1797 BC). I've been out there several times."

Curiosity made my voice waiver as I asked: "Were you in the underground rooms? After all, there were supposedly 1,500 of them."

Adel shrugged his shoulders and shook his head: "There are no underground rooms. A few recesses with smaller walls and a number of smaller chambers, that's all. No labyrinthine corridors, let alone reliefs or lavish art."

"Adel!" I put my crossed arms on the table top and stared straight into his face. "Even if you didn't go underground, the rooms above should have astounded you. Remember: Herodotus wrote of walls full of reliefs, of twelve covered courtyards with huge carved figures, and of a pyramid with huge figures carved into it. He assured his readers that he had seen the upper buildings with his own eyes, and that they were 'almost superhuman work,' surpassing even the pyramids. And don't forget Strabo, who reported gigantic ceilings made of stone. All of this, including the marble columns, cannot have vanished into thin air."

Unsettled by my vehemence, Adel stared at the table top and nervously ran his hands over it. Then he replied: "I can only repeat what we were taught at the University of Vienna. Incidentally, the local antiquities administration tells the same story—that the labyrinth is located at the pyramid of Amenemhet III." Then, after some hesitation, he said: "But you have now confused me with your evidence from ancient historians. There are indeed unbelievable discrepancies here."

We kept silent for a few moments. And then it became clear to me that I had to go to the oasis of El Fayoum myself and see the pyramid of Amenemhet III with my own eyes. If the labyrinth had been on the shores of Lake Moeris, did the El Fayoum oasis lie on or near the remains of that artificial lake? Were there still remains of canals with mighty locks?

Pondering my decision, I asked Adel if the pyramid of Amenemhet III was in the desert. He replied that it was and asked why that mattered.

"It may," I answered. "Thousands of years ago, when the labyrinth stood, the desert may have been green fertile land, with canals and a lake larger than Lake Constance. The climate could have changed completely since then."

Thirty-four years *after* our talks about the Egyptian labyrinth, science confirmed my suspicions. An international team of ten natural scientists examined the climatic conditions in the Sahara. Experts from many distinguished universities worked on the joint project, among them the Laboratoire Géosciences at the Université Paris-Sud; the Department of Earth, Atmospheric, and Planetary Sciences at the Massachusetts Institute of Technology; the Lamont-Doherty Earth Observatory and the Department of Earth and Environmental Sciences at Columbia University; the Laboratoire d'Océanologie et de Géoscience at the Université de Lille in France; the Department of Environmental Studies at Macalester College in Minnesota; the GAIA-Antarctica Project at the Universidad de Magallanes in Chile; and the Université de Bordeaux in France.

But what did these experts hope to find? What justified such a high level of scientific effort?

FROM GARDEN TO DESERT

It is generally known that the Sahara must have been green at some point in time. For decades, fossils of ungulates—animals that could not have survived without green fodder—have repeatedly been uncovered in the Sahara, including in Libya and Egypt. Rock carvings also show hoofed animals. But how could a parched desert environment develop from a green and fertile landscape? What could cause such radical climate change?

The international team investigating climate change in the Sahara published their findings in the January 2019 issue of the journal *Science Advances*.[22] They concluded that carbon dioxide had nothing to do with the climate change in the Sahara, but that radical climate change *did* occur. Moreover, they were able to prove beyond a doubt that it occurs in 20,000-year cycles by analyzing layers of dust that had accumulated in the Sahara over the past 240,000 years. When they bored holes in the ground and examined the different layers found in the core, they could clearly demonstrate these climate changes. The changes, they concluded, resulted from changes in the tilt of the Earth's axis that affected the distribution of sunlight.

To understand this, you have to know that the Earth is not a perfect sphere. Because of its rotation, it is slightly flattened at the poles and thicker at the equator than it is from pole to pole. In addition, the Earth's axis is inclined at an angle of 23.5 degrees relative to the perpendicular of what's called the "ecliptic," which defines the level at which the Earth orbits the sun. Because the Earth is not a perfect sphere, it behaves like a child's spinning top; it wobbles. In astronomy, this movement is called "precession." Because of this wobble, the constellations we see in the sky change position over the course of 25,800 years.

At the beginning of spring, the sun is presently positioned in front of the constellation Pisces. In 6,450 years, it will be positioned in front of Sagittarius. In 12,900 years, it will stand in front of Virgo and, in 19,350 years, it will be positioned in front of Gemini. This shift in the Earth's axis is the reason for our seasons. Because of the wobbling of our planet, the radiation of the sunlight is not evenly distributed over the different continents, and this changes every century. In terms of the Sahara, if the intensity of the radiation from the sun increases, this results in increased monsoon activity in the region, which leads to a wetter, and therefore greener, Sahara. If the sun's radiation is reduced due to the inclination of the Earth's axis, the monsoon activity is diminished and a drier climate is created.

So the Egyptian labyrinth *could* have stood in green fields thousands of years ago, on the shore of a large lake like Lake Moeris. When the climate changed, the vegetation died and the wind transported dust and sand across the landscape, burying the labyrinth with its gigantic ceiling stones and marble columns and large figures under layers of desert soil. Lake Moeris dried up. After all, the famous Sphinx in front of the Great Pyramid was hidden under a thick layer of sand for centuries and has been excavated again and again.

THE HAWARA SITE

In the summer of 1988, Adel and I drove out to the pyramid of Amenemhet III. Adel had rented a four-wheel-drive all-terrain vehicle that was in amazingly good condition. We made our way to Giza, humming along busy noisy streets, past the Great Pyramids, taking a southwesterly route directly into the desert. The road that leads in a straight line to the oasis of El Fayoum, as if drawn with a ruler, is paved, so it turns out that we really didn't need an all-terrain vehicle.

To the right and left of the 106-kilometer road, we repeatedly came across the hulls of scrapped vehicles. Adel explained that the Bedouins used to ride to the oasis by camel, but today they travel by car. When vehicles break down, which happens often in the harsh desert environment, they are abandoned on the side of the road, but only after every last part and piece of upholstery is stripped and carted away. I thought of Herodotus as we passed these abandonned vehicles. He could only have covered the distance from the pyramids in Giza to Hawara by camel—a two-day trip. Or perhaps he traveled by boat, since he had described navigable canals.

Finally, after a two-hour drive, glistening streaks of water appeared on the horizon. Adel explained that the El Fayoum oasis was surrounded by desert, but that today, the area was artificially irrigated. As the chant of a prayer came across on the car radio, Adel bowed to the east, saying that a top Sunni cleric was asking the believers to pray to Allah for water. In the summer of 1988, Ethiopia was suffereing from its seventh year of drought. No rain, no Nile water; no Nile water, no muddy canals; no canals, no agriculture. I asked Adel about the Nasser Dam that had been built above Aswan.

"The water level of the dam has dropped by twenty-five meters in the past three years," he lamented. "If it doesn't rain in Sudan or Ethiopia in the next two months, the turbines of the dam will have to be shut down. This is bad because many now depend on the electric power the dam provides. When the Nile cannot feed the thousands of canals to the right and left of the river, the fields dry up. A catastrophe for the fifty-six million Egyptians. Almost three million hectares of fields are irrigated in Egypt and this requires almost fifty billion cubic meters of water. Without the Nile waters, the whole country would be in serious trouble."

After driving ninety kilometers, we saw the first green patches starting to appear on the side of the road. Merchants waved and children held out flower bouquets, onions and garlic knotted together in garlands, and even live chickens and turkeys. Then I saw the first canal, with happy, naked children splashing about in the slow-moving muddy waters.

Cotton fields appeared, alternating with corn, cauliflower, and sugar cane. Women sat in front of mud houses, some of them weaving baskets while others made bowls; delicate children's hands painted the products in bright colors. Adel said that they were godly, honest, and frugal people whose families cultivated the fields every year, working from sunrise to sunset. When the first stone houses came into view, Adel explained that this was el-Medina, the capital of the oasis, which had originally been called Crocodile City. Today, the place was popularly called El Fayoum.

"Strabo wrote about a Crocodile City," I mused. "He described it as being on the shore of a lake and said that his innkeeper threw dry bread to a crocodile."

"That doesn't mean anything," said Adel, and the corners of his mouth twisted into a crooked grin. "There were countless Crocodile Cities in ancient Egypt. El Fayoum is only one of them. The god Sobek was worshiped in the form of a crocodile in every major temple. He is often depicted wearing a double crown, but sometimes with a falcon's head. Sobek was also considered the god of water. Whenever the Nile flooded its banks, entire herds of crocodiles frolicked in the shallow water. People believed that the water itself was the sweat of the crocodiles. When Seth murdered his brother, Osiris, he dismembered him and threw his body parts into the water. It was Sobek who retrieved them and put Osiris back together."

About ten kilometers southeast of the village of Hawara, I saw the first outline of a dark gray triangle—the pyramid of Amenemhet III. It reminded me of a flattened pudding with a few dents in it (see Figures 16 and 17). We were the only visitors at the site. In front of the pyramid was a black-framed sign that read: Labyrinth/305 × 244 meters/3000 rooms. A lonely guard, who had been awakened by our engine noise, joined us. Adel talked to him and showed his ID as a state tour guide. I added a £20 note and he let us through.

Adel and I poked around the site for at least four hours. We climbed over small walls from Ptolemaic and Roman times and, with the help of my strong flashlight, we crawled into shafts and through chambers. The only thing we saw that might have been a former temple was a few chunks of reddish Aswan granite. There were no remains of stone slabs of extraordinary size, as Strabo had reported. There were no traces of the large blocks of

Figures 16 and 17. The pyramid of Amenemhet III at Hawara.

syenite that Pliny had observed, let alone the remains of
the "almost superhuman" work at which Herodotus had
marveled. Nothing but barren walls and rubble. No walls
full of reliefs. No huge figures carved on a pyramid. No
remains of two other pyramids that might previously have

looked out over Lake Moeris. What we saw gave us no indication that something had stood there that was larger than the great pyramids.

Together, Adel and I climbed the pyramid of Amenemhet III, panting in the hot dry air, our shirts sticking to our chests. The whole structure, which had partially disintegrated, consisted of black mud bricks that had initially been made by pressing clay and mud between boards and then air-drying them (see Figure 17). I was looking for something extraordinary—for a granite ledge that could have borne the burden of "giant figures" in Herodotus' time. But there was nothing to be found. The pyramid had partially disintegrated, and Adel explained that the residents of the area had broken mud bricks out of its walls to use for their houses. There was no trace of the limestone that had originally covered the structure. Rain had carved furrows into the mountain of mud bricks, washing out large chunks, some of them as long as fifty centimeters. I photographed several broken bricks in which we could see straw, dried grass, and small stones.

The pyramid itself stands fifty-eight meters high and is flattened at the top. Below us, we saw a few walls and sand mounds. Farther in the distance, we saw high-voltage pylons and a thin canal that cut diagonally through the surrounding farmland. But nowhere did we see the remains of a navigable canal with gigantic locks that Herodotus and others claimed to have observed. No 1,500 rooms above ground, never mind an equal number below ground. No walls full of reliefs that had amazed ancient visitors.

I thought of the colorful reliefs on the temple walls of the monument to Seti I in Abydos. Like the pyramid of Amenemhet III, these were also more than 3,000 years old, and yet they had survived all the storms of history and the weather. Where were the Parian stones about which Pliny had exclaimed? Where were the inextricable, confusing corridors that wore him out? And even if the formerly huge Lake Moeris had dried up completely, where were the remains of the two pyramids that Herodotus reported, each of which rose fifty fathoms out of the water and reached just as deeply into it? Structures like these do not just disappear into thin air, even after thousands of years.

I also remembered that every pharaoh was proud of his accomplishments and wanted to preserve them to prove his importance to posterity. If Amenemhet III had been the builder of the labyrinth we sought, then indestructible inscriptions would have celebrated his own deeds and praised the builder of the monument and showered him with honor. None of this can be found at Hawara.

With our all-terrain vehicle, we explored the whole area, eventually leaving the streets and dirt roads behind and venturing out into the desert. We searched for the shorelines of the vanished Lake Moeris, which Herodotus claims was a human marvel of 3,600 stadia and with a coastline as long as that of Egypt. We didn't find anything—no navigable canals, no remains of the mighty locks that had still existed in Strabo's time. Nothing. If the Romans, or later, the Christians, had known about the labyrinth, there should have been a record. Any author of the past 2,000 years would have been informed about it. And yet all we find in the record refers to the destruction of great libraries. But the works of art and the colorful reliefs from a total of 3,000 rooms could not have disappeared without a trace. At least remnants of these phenomenal reliefs, engravings, and figures would be represented in museums or private collections. And yet there is no trace of any of it.

This leads me to believe that the labyrinth still lies undiscovered somewhere under the sands of the Egyptian desert. In fact, it is quite possible that modern aerial archeology has actually found traces of the underground rooms of the Egyptian labyrinth, although this has never been acknowledged. It is possible that researchers and others simply don't want to talk about these discoveries because there is no money for excavations. Or perhaps they are reticent to share their discoveries because the sheer abundance of information that could be obtained from the labyrinth would upset our current knowledge of the early history of mankind, in the same way that the chambers in and under the Great Pyramid did.

SEARCH FOR THE LABYRINTH

After our trip to the pyramid of Amenemhet III, Adel and I sat with dusty, sweaty hair and stubbly beards at the bar in the Hotel Meridian just under a kilometer from the pyramid of Cheops. Once again, I wondered if Adel or the clan of grave robbers had visited individual rooms in the labyrinth without actually understanding what they had found. When I put the question to him, Adel responded with a question of his own: "Why are we archeologists taught that Richard Lepsius discovered the labyrinth, yet when we go there, nothing matches what he claims he saw?"

At that time, in the summer of 1988, I had no answer for him. But a few weeks later, I buried myself in the special literature, trying to find out why the entire professional community believed that the German researcher Richard Lepsius had discovered the Egyptian labyrinth. Below, I outline what I published on the subject.[23]

Richard Lepsius, the son of a district administrator from Naumburg on the river Saale, was considered a genius. He was an eccentric, authoritative, and enthusiastic man who was able to read Egyptian hieroglyphs and was the first to notice that these were not just abbreviations, but that they also represented phonetic and syllabic signs. Based on his in-depth knowledge, he authored several publications on ancient Egypt in the 1830s. In 1842, on behalf of His Majesty King Friedrich Wilhelm IV, he led an expedition to the distant land on the Nile. Lepsius was very politically aware and didn't mind raising the Prussian flag on the pyramid of Cheops on the King's birthday and playing the Prussian national anthem in the King's Chamber.

Lepsius was familiar with the writings of Herodotus, Strabo, and others, and had set his mind on finding the mysterious labyrinth. He was convinced that Lake Karun, which lies twenty-five kilometers northwest of the oasis of El Fayoum, was the former Lake Moeris described by ancient authors. Diodorus of Sicily had reported that the builder of the labyrinth was named Mendes, "whom some also call Marrhos," which was also the throne name of Amenemhet III, who had the pyramid built in Hawara. Moreover, because El Fayoum had formerly been called Crocodile City, Lepsius felt important connections to the site did exist.

On May 23, 1843, Lepsius wrote: "We camped in Faium at the ruins of the labyrinth. Its location had long been correctly suspected there; and the very first glance left us with no doubt about it."[24] His bias was even more clearly expressed in the letters he sent to faraway Berlin:

> We have been here on the south side of the pyramid of Moeris since May 23, on top of the ruins of the labyrinth. Because it was clear from the first moment that we had the full right to use this term as soon as I had a brief look at it all. I didn't believe it would be so easy for us to be convinced.[25]

Lepsius was by no means the first to search for the labyrinth at the El Fayoum oasis. The French explorer Paul Lucas had already pitched his tent on Lake Karun in 1714, because he assumed that the remains of the two pyramids, whose tips protruded above the water in Herodotus' time, should be visible there. Of course, he found no trace of them.

In January 1801, P. D. Martin, an engineer of Napoleon's Egyptian army, rode across the desert to the

El Fayoum oasis. He also suspected that the labyrinth was located there, but found nothing. In 1828, Charles X of France (1757–1836) commissioned the translator of the hieroglyphs, Jean-François Champollion, to lead an expedition to Egypt. Champollion also searched for the labyrinth to no avail. Finally, just one year before Lepsius, a French research group reached the pyramid of Amenemhet III. They found a few walls and broken pillars lying around, but there was no sign of the remains of a gigantic building complex.

Enter Richard Lepsius, who brought his good name to the search for the labyrinth. He had a fine reputation and the archaeological world trusted him. After he announced that the labyrinth was at the pyramid in Hawara, it seemed that no further search for the lost miracle was necessary. On closer inspection, however, nothing at all that he found matched the statements of the ancient writers and historians. Lepsius had trenches dug in five different places and, after a few days, he had exposed some remains of granite and limestone pillars that shimmered "almost like marble." But Herodotus had described carefully assembled white marble columns. The enthusiastic Prussian found "hundreds of adjacent and superimposed chambers, small ones next to larger ones . . . without any regularly occurring entrances and exits, so that the description of Herodotus and Strabo in this regard seemed to be completely justified."

Really?

Where are the intertwined, crooked paths reported by Strabo? And where are the huge ceilings built of a single slab of stone? Where are the concealed passageways and the slabs of stone of extraordinary size? Where are the twelve roofed courtyards with gates that face each other? Where are the giant, carved figures of which Herodotus wrote? Lepsius personally testified that he had "discovered no inscriptions." Herodotus, however, was amazed by walls full of reliefs.

Two thousands years ago, Pliny reported descending to galleries on ninety steps. If you allow a height of only twenty centimeters per step, these galleries would have been about eighteen meters below what was then the ground-floor level. But there was no sign of any of this at Lepsius's find. Pliny spoke of houses in arched halls underground, but Lepsius never entered houses in underground halls, nor does he claim that any graves or sarcophagi of pharaohs were discovered by his expedition.

Herodotus reported finding a pyramid of fifty fathoms "at the corner at the end of the labyrinth," into which huge figures were carved. The eyewitness Strabo describes a square pyramid about four plethra on each side. According to Herodotus, the sides of the pyramid measured seventy-one meters; according to Strabo, they measured 120 meters. But the sides of the pyramid of Amenemhet III in Hawara measure 106 meters. And it is possible that none of these numbers are correct. Herodotus and Strabo agree that this pyramid is "at a corner" at the end of the labyrinth. But that doesn't fit any location on the Hawara site. The pyramid of Amenemhet III is not located at a corner at all, but on the same axis as the walls.

Moreover, Herodotus reports that giant figures were carved into the pyramid. But these are nowhere to be found at Hawara for the simple reason that the Hawara pyramid is made of mud bricks. You can't carve figures into dried mud bricks, let alone giant ones. The material is much too soft for that. Although the Hawara pyramid is said to have originally been covered with limestone slabs, that doesn't change things. These limestone slabs would have to have been anchored onto the mud bricks. But that would be like trying to anchor a ten-meter-high granite equestrian statue in a bowl of porridge. The ancient historians wrote of almost superhuman work (Herodotus), structures impossible to surpass (Diodorus), and buildings that consisted of large blocks of syenite (Pliny). But the Hawara pyramid of Pharaoh Amenemhet III consists only of mud bricks. *Facta loquuntur*—facts speak for themselves.

And there is something else.

Lepsius discovered nameplates of Amenemhet III in a chamber. From this, he drew the correct conclusion: "We now know for certain who the builder and owner of the pyramid is."[26] Forty-five years later, British archaeologist Flinders Petrie (1853–1942) did indeed find the intact sarcophagi of Amenemhet III and his daughter inside the pyramid. The burial chamber consisted of a yellow block of quartzite that was lowered into the ground. Finally, sewer workers came across a 1.60-meter-high limestone statue of the seated Amenemhet III nearby. But none of the hieroglyphs on these finds proclaimed that Amenemhet III was the builder of a labyrinth or that his pyramid stood over one. Flinders Petrie is said to have found the burial chamber of Amenemhet III untouched. But it is absolutely inconceivable that the pharaoh would not have had a glyph placed somewhere mentioning the labyrinth if, in fact, he had built one.

And why did Lepsius, who had five trenches dug in the same place and explored the Hawara pyramid down to the last corner, not find the burial chamber and statue of Amenemhet III? I contend that is because he did his research superficially, because he was biased.

It is astonishing that the pyramid of Amenemhet III is the only structure in all of Egypt's archeological literature that is identified as the building under which the labyrinth lies. Richard Lepsius' claim to have discovered the labyrinth is mentioned by scholars everywhere. It seems to me, however, that these scholars climb a spiral staircase without ever looking back. Every new researcher takes over the nonsense put forth by the previous one. In fact, it has long been known that several of the walls and chambers that Lepsius had excavated by his workers and by children actually date from Roman and even Greek times. Amenemhet III was just the builder of the mud-brick pyramid and possibly some structures around it. The whole site has about as much in common with Herodotus' description of the labyrinth as pop music has with Beethoven's Fifth.

And we haven't yet said a word about Lake Moeris, which Herodotus claims was a human miracle that measured 3,600 stadia. Diodorus of Sicily gives the same account and supplements Herodotus' statement: "He also had a lake dug ten schoeni from here, in the area above the city, of extraordinary usefulness and of unbelievable size. Its size is said to be 3,600 stadia and the depth in most places is fifty fathoms." And according to ancient historians, the labyrinth, the pyramids, and the lake belong together.

But geologists today have determined that there was never a lake at the Hawara pyramid by analyzing the soil deposits found there.[27] And consider that the pyramid of Amenemhet III was made from mud bricks, which are not compatible with water at all. A foundation built of mud bricks would have softened, flooding the underground chambers with groundwater. Thus, the Hawara pyramid could not have stood on the shores of Lake Moeris. Today, the shallow Lake Karun lies twenty-five kilometers northwest of El Fayoum, but this lake can't be the Lake Moeris described by Herodotus and other writers—not just because it is located forty kilometers in a straight line from the Hawara pyramid, but also because it is a natural lake that is not fed by canals. Moreover, Lepsius examined the shores of this lake and searched for the two pyramids, but he found nothing, writing resignedly: "The statements that the labyrinth and the capital Arsinoe [Crocodile City] were located on its banks [Lake Karun] are just as inaccurate."

The statements of Richard Lepsius and those of ancient historians about distances cannot be reconciled either. Diodorus of Sicily confirmed that King Moeris had the artificial lake dug ten schoeni above the city of Memphis. But Memphis is located twenty-four kilometers southwest of Cairo and is considered the oldest city in Egypt, founded during the First Dynasty by Menes (also called Meni, and equated with Hor Aha) sometime around 3000 BC. This Menes built the first temple of the god Ptah, considered the creator god and god of the arts, west of the Nile. Later, Amenemhet III as well as Sethos I and rulers from the Ramses dynasties had phenomenal temples erected in Memphis.

Today, tourists marvel at the sculpturally perfect statues of Ramses. But Memphis lies seventy kilometers due northeast of Hawara. Moreover, Herodotus specified, in the fourth chapter of his second book:

> *The present country north of Lake Moeris did not protrude from it at that time, whereas now one must drive up the river to Lake Moeris for seven days . . . The locals say that the lake has an underground run-off to the Libyan river Syrte, which flows west into the country, along the mountains above Memphis.*

So Herodotus's labyrinth would have to be a little farther up beyond Lake Moeris. And this geographical description in no way fits the location of the pyramid of Amenemhet III in Hawara.

For these reasons and more, I believe the Egyptian labyrinth still lies undiscovered in the Egyptian desert— probably somewhere "along the mountains above Memphis" (Herodotus). But Memphis is also very close to the Saqqara pyramid. And that's where the search leads next.

CHAPTER 4

Adel's Strange Tale

THREE DAYS AFTER OUR TRIP to Hawara, Adel and I met in the bar at the Mena House Hotel and talked again about the lost labyrinth. Adel said that he still had to drive home across Cairo, so we decided not to have anything to drink. Remembering our previous conversations, I asked him what had happened when he was lost under the Saqqara pyramid. After hesitating for a moment or two, Adel asked me to switch off my tape recorder but said that I could take notes.

"What I experienced back then is simply impossible," Adel began, "that's why I never talk about it. What would you say, for example, if I told you I had lost my virginity to a ghost that doesn't really exist?" He planted both of his arms firmly on the table and looked me in the eye, as if waiting for an answer to his strange question. At first, I was silent. Then I crossed my arms, put on a serious expression, and turned to face him.

"Because it is you and because we trust each other with a lot of confidential information, I'd want to hear your story and then I'd think about it for a long time. You know I never accept the word 'impossible' at face value."

At first, Adel said nothing more, then I heard him take a few deep breaths. Obviously, he was struggling with his feelings.

"Erich, I can never forget anything that happened to me on that stange day. Today, I am fifty-seven years old. On June 6, 1944, I was just sixteen—a boy who knew nothing of politics. I had been lucky enough to attend a private school and knew that Egypt was ruled by King Faruk I (1936–1952). I knew that World War II was raging in distant Europe and that the British were caught up in it. I faintly remember hearing about a tank battle that took place in the desert of El Alamein in which thousands of German soldiers fell to British superiority. But we children were hardly interested in all of this.

"My grandfather had been a physician," Adel explained. "He owned some land that my father later sold in order to open a small shop with his brother in which they sold souvenirs and antiques. But tourism hadn't really begun to flourish yet in Egypt and our family had to keep looking for new sources of income. So we turned to trafficking in antiquities. There was no shortage of buyers who were looking for artifacts from Egypt for museums and wealthy families, and those buyers paid well.

Sometimes we even dealt in fake certificates. The size of the artifacts did not matter. Gentleman buyers, as I call them today, easily shipped huge statues to Europe and the United States.

"At the beginning of March 1944," he went on, "my father and his brother were digging around an artificial wall behind which they suspected lay an old tomb. My twenty-eight-year-old cousin and I were standing guard. We wore the traditional *jalabiya*—a shirt that goes down to the ankles. Although Egyptian boys usually don't wear much under this shirt except perhaps some type of pubic wrapping, my cousin and I always wore long cotton pants underneath—a kind of forerunner of blue jeans. We wore no socks, just sandals that could be tied with a shoelace."

"Where did you search?" I asked.

"In many places," he replied, "but these events took place in Saqqara, not far from the step pyramid."

And then Adel embarked on one of the strangest stories I had ever heard. I summarize it here from memory and from my notes.

INTO THE CRYPT

"Today, a paved road goes by Saqqara and tourist buses use it to reach the entrance to the excavation complex," Adel began, "but back then we approached the site on a dirt road. My cousin was about seventy meters below where my father and his brother were digging; I was about seventy meters above them. Suddenly, I heard my father screaming and saw his brother waving us over. A stone block had jammed his left arm and pinned it as tightly as in a vise. We tried to lift it, but it didn't move.

"As my father groaned and grimaced, his brother told my cousin to run to the forecourt and get help. Ten minutes later, there were six of us trying to free my father. One of the pyramid guards had a crowbar with him and managed to move the rectangular block of sandstone far enough so that my father could pull out his arm. It had turned blue and was broken. Because my grandfather had been a physician, we still had good relationships with local doctors, and one of them set my father's broken bones without asking too many questions.

"That same evening, my family all sat in the large common room enjoying *muluchija*—a spicy stew in which you can put anything. My father had taken something for the pain—a natural remedy, because other medicines weren't available at the time. I remember him asking everybody to be calm, pointing to his cast and solemnly saying: 'It was worth it.' Then he explained that, behind the wall in which his arm had gotten stuck, he had found an undamaged grave. Through the small gap in the wall, he had seen hieroglyphs and a lot of shiny objects. As soon as his wound was healed, he said, we would try to drill an opening into the chamber. And that was how my incomparable adventure began."

As Adel paused, I recommended that he lower his voice, as I feared being overheard. When I ordered a glass of wine, Adel refused. He wasn't going to drink anything, he said, but the alcohol might help me get through his story. Then we smoked together in silence, until Adel leaned forward and returned to his tale, speaking slowly and in a soft voice.

"When we returned to the site," he said, "we only worked after 5 P.M. when there was no one else there except us. Since there were no tourists at that hour, there were hardly any guards either. We brought chisels, crowbars, spades, shovels, hammers in different sizes, pickaxes, and two jacks, like the ones used to lift cars. We also brought flashlights with spare batteries, a few bandages, and big towels that we could wrap around our heads to protect our mouths and noses from dust and from poisons that we might inhale. We knew from the story of the curse of the pharaohs that the deceased may have protected their graves with some kind of poison thousands of years ago. And of course we had a canister of drinking water with us. We left our car parked behind a small hill just a few meters from our excavation site.

"The really hard work was done by my father and his brother. As before, my cousin and I stood guard. When they had cut an opening through the rock and secured the top rock with a jack, they called us over. But the rectangular block above turned out to be granite, and it didn't move an inch. I was the slimmest one in the group, and my father said I should crawl into the hole backward. Once I was inside, he handed me one of the large cloths to wrap around my head and a flashlight, and told me

I was to stay close enough to the hole so that they could still see me from the outside.

"When I first shined my flashlight at the walls, I saw a winged sun disk that I recognized from the friezes of several temples. Its golden colors reflected off the wall. My father wanted to know if I saw a sarcophagus, but there was none. However, I saw two gilded chests with hieroglyphs and representations on them that I didn't understand at all. Excitedly, I shouted my discoveries to those waiting outside, and my father said that under no circumstances was I to open the chests.

"'What else do you see?' my father shouted. The beam of my flashlight fell next on a green eye of Horus, something I had learned about in school and recognized from temple walls. My light finally illuminated a scene that depicted a group of brown-skinned children all staring at a starry sky. They wore cloths around their abdomens and were barefoot. Then I noticed an opening on the left that seemed to lead into a shaft. My father forbade me to go in that direction and ordered me to crawl back out. But I never got back to the hole.

"Suddenly the passage around me cracked and crackled as if the ceiling above me were about to collapse. I heard my father and his brother scream, threw myself into a corner, and put my arms protectively over my head. Then all fell silent. A few smaller stones rolled off the ceiling. The daylight from the hole I had crawled in through was no longer visible; I could see only a faint ray of light through a small gap very close to where it had been. I could hear my father's voice and those of the others, so I put my lips to where the opening had been and shouted that I was okay. My father replied quickly, asking if I was hurt. I felt my body. No wounds, no abrasions, nothing.

"My father shouted that he would slide a flashlight battery through the gap and smaller bottles of drinking water, but that I should use them sparingly. They would go to get help and get me out. Using a piece of wood, he pushed the battery and bottles of water through the small gap. I drank one bottle immediately and pushed it back out the same way. My father pushed in two more bottles, saying that that was all they had. He told me that the ceiling had collapsed, and that the jack was crushed. They were dealing with granite, and would need heavy equipment to get me out.

"Keeping the grave site secret was no longer important. Now it was all about my life. My father suggested that I try to get some sleep and told me not to enter the tunnel I had told them about. It could be tomorrow before they returned, he warned me. Then he shouted that he loved me and that I shouldn't be afraid.

"Strange, but I didn't feel any fear. I crouched down on the floor with my legs crossed. When I aimed the flashlight beam at the walls, I saw a relief of a cobra staring directly at me. The snake had a golden body adorned with dark red stones on both sides. Its oversized eyes and head were made of green material. I saw other figures wearing dark-brown make-up, with big eyes. There were hieroglyphs and zigzag lines to the side of them. One image was of a person with a golden headband and a beard lying on a bed. A dead body or a sick person? I couldn't tell. Leaning over the person was a jackal-headed figure that was touching the body. It was only years later that I learned that the jackal was named Anubis, and that he was the god responsible for mummification.

"On the wall to my right, I saw reliefs with agricultural themes—oxen stomping grain and people lined up with flails in their hands. Next to them, the goddess Hathor appeared with the cattle horns and the sun disk on top of her hair. All these images and more glowed in bright colors, as if the artists had just put their tools down yesterday. It was in that burial chamber that I wished for the first time that I could understand the gods and read the hieroglyphs.

"After a time, I shined my light into the left corner, where I saw a dark opening—the one my father had told me not to enter. But the uncertainty bothered me. What was in there? Was I in any danger from the opening? Eventually, my curiosity won out and I approached the corner. In it, I found a staircase that was wide enough for two people to walk side by side. Later, many years later, I saw something similar when visiting some tombs in the Valley of the Kings.

"About twenty steps down this staircase, I came to a flat floor and, above me, I saw an arched ceiling with oversized, winged-sun drawings. Between them there was a dark-blue field decorated with yellow-gold stars and a picture of a heavenly barge, similar to one I found in the hall of the temple of Dendera thirty years later [see color insert]. Less than two meters in front of me stood a wooden chair with side arms and a backrest. It seemed completely incongruous, as if it had been left there by accident. It had no inscriptions, no drawings, and no engravings on it—just a nameless armchair. I checked its strength with my hands and elbows, and then hesitantly sat on it.

"And that was when the first miracle began."

THE GLOWING CHAMBER

"Gently, as if asking for permission, various stones in the walls began to glow. First, it was a dark-red glow, like that of charcoal burning out. Then it turned orange. I stared at the walls and didn't dare to move. The orange color turned into a soft yellow, and it stayed that way. It was not the walls themselves that glowed, but only isolated stones in them. A soft brightness covered the entire room. It was only decades later that I read the pyramid chapter in the ancient book *Hitat* that described glowing stones that were used in the construction of pyramids, brought here from the East. Stones like these are also mentioned in Arabic fairy tales, where they are called *andaran*. The stones looked like lamps glowing in the dark.

"As I looked around, I found myself in a square room with a ceiling blanketed in stars and walls covered in images of barges. There was a gilded chest in the middle of the room, and a falcon with folded wings sat on it.

I stared at the bird and couldn't shake the feeling that it was watching me. No matter which way I moved my torso, the falcon's eyes followed. I slid the chair forward about two meters and the bird's eyes moved with me. I moved back again, and the bird always turned toward me, as if it were alive, although I knew that was impossible. For the first time, I felt fear creep quietly up inside of me. I had heard of mummified birds—for example, the ibis we had seen as school children when visiting the Egyptian Museum. But this falcon wasn't a mummy.

"To build up my courage, I slowly turned the chair around. On the back wall, where the staircase had led into the room, I found colored reliefs of different deities wearing complicated crowns. At first, the only one I recognized was an image of Thoth as a young man with a bird's face, a crescent moon, and a ball over his head. But then I saw Horus greeting me with the winged sun disk. He didn't appear only on the back wall, but also on the ceiling (see color insert). Six red figures were squatting on one side wall, each holding a candle-like object in its left hand. In front of them stood a figure in a white cloak that seemed to be conducting the "candle bearers" like an orchestra leader. On the opposite wall were two tall people—one with brown skin, the other with green skin and a falcon's head.

"In between them appeared an even larger figure with a white petticoat and a white cape over it. Woman or man? I couldn't tell. The figure had black hair that reached to the shoulders and a white headband. The people flanking

The Mortuary Temple of Hatshepsut,
located on the west bank of the Nile
near the Valley of the Kings.

The Mortuary Temple of Hatshepsut,
located on the west bank of the Nile
near the Valley of the Kings.

Model of the Valley of the Kings.

Ruins of Minoan Palace in Knossos.

Ruins of Minoan Palace in Knossos.

Divine Apis bulls with sun disks between their horns.

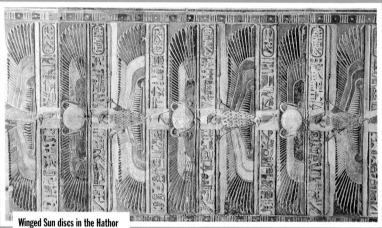

Winged Sun discs in the Hathor
temple in Dendera.

Winged Sun discs in the Hathor
temple in Dendera.

The Serapheum in Sakkara with
the gigantic sarcophaguses.

The Serapheum in Sakkara with
the gigantic sarcophaguses.

Tunnels and entrances to the underground in Sakkara.

Tunnels and entrances to the underground in Sakkara.

Avenue of the sphinxes in Luxor.

Procession of the gods on the temple roof in Dendera.

Crop circles in Sainte-Hippolyte, France (Summer 2019).

Crop circles in Sainte-Hippolyte, France (Summer 2019).

it on both sides held a kind of protective chain over its head that consisted of nothing but ankh signs [life signs], with which I was also familiar from my museum visits. And there were hieroglyphs on all the walls.

"In one corner of the room stood a sofa-like frame—like a bed without a backrest—that was covered with a dark-red brocade blanket. I could see multicolored, thick threads that were woven through the brocade. I immediately thought of the Kaaba in Mecca, the most important sanctuary in Islam, whose walls are hung with pure brocade.

"Since the shining stones in the wall had begun to glow when I sat in the chair, I decided to determine whether they would continue to glow if I got up from it. I got up several times and sat down again, but nothing happened—although the falcon's head followed my movements. I cautiously walked toward the sofa, hesitated, and finally worked up the courage to lie down on it. The bed reminded me of my mattress at home—not too soft, as if it had been stuffed with dried straw. The room was beginning to fascinate me. I felt astonishing joy. I forgot all about my father and his warnings, rolled my headscarf behind my neck, and closed my eyes."

MAHLINJA

"Suddenly, although minutes may have passed, I felt a touch on my cheek. I shot up, startled, and heard a calming voice that said: 'Don't be afraid, Adel. I was wait-ing for you.' Then I saw the most incredibly beautiful girl in the world kneeling beside me. Never in my entire fifty-seven years have I ever seen anything so perfect. She seemed to be about my age. A bluish-colored, very trans-parent veil hung around her body. I was sixteen and had never seen a naked female before. Not even a girl's naked breasts, let alone anything more. But this was real. Not a dream, not my imagination.

"The girl knelt next to the sofa and ran her fingers through my hair. With gentle, soulful movements, she stroked my eyebrows, then leaned over me and kissed my eyes. And then she smiled. Simply perfect. Indescrib-able. How to describe such incredible beauty? Her dark pupils were set off against the whites of her eyes. I could tell immediately that she wore no make-up. Her eye-brows looked like those of a divine creature. Her nose was in perfect proportion to her enchanting face—her nostrils neither wide nor narrow. She reminded me of the virgins that my Muslim schoolmates had told me were promised in the holy Koran to the righteous in the heavenly realms after death. Was I dead and in heaven?

"'You are alive, Adel,' replied the voice, as if reading my mind. 'I was waiting for you.'

"I hesitated, before daring to ask: 'Who are you?'

"'Where I come from, my name is Mahlinja,' she answered.

"'Are you alive?' I asked bravely.

"'You can feel my body,' she smiled. Then she wrapped her long scarf around my neck and covered my entire face with caresses."

Adel paused. But his story had taken hold of me. Was it a fabrication? Was it a dream? I urged him to go on, and encouraged him to tell me everything.

"Everything?" he asked with a trembling voice. "Even the most intimate details?"

"Yes, please. I haven't got my recorder on and haven't made a single note yet."

Adel pushed a burning candle aside and asked the waiter for an empty ashtray. Then he ordered in Arabic that we not be disturbed and picked up his story where he had left off.

"Mahlinja opened the two buttons on my jalabiya," he said hesitantly. "Her hands caressed my breast. Gently, as if to ask permission, she pulled up my shirt. I pulled it over my head and threw it on the floor. I was just sixteen and completely inexperienced sexually. No one had ever seen my penis, let alone touched it. That was an absolute taboo. And now Mahlinja's lips, her tongue, her hands, even her teeth, seemed to be everywhere at the same time. We made passionate love, our arms and legs entwined. We giggled like silly children as we explored each other's bodies, overcome by waves of tenderness. It was like nothing I had ever known before. When we fell back exhausted, she knelt beside the sofa and covered my chest with caresses and, as she kissed my eyes, in my mind I heard her voice say that she had to go back.

"My mind teemed with questions. Back to where? How did she know my name? Why had she been waiting for me? But I couldn't seem to articulate the questions; my voice failed me.

"Mahlinja got up, carefully put her blue veil around her shoulders, took a few steps back from the sofa, and smiled. Her teeth were flawless and her lips were those of an angel, created by God himself. In the dimly lit room, her blue veil looked blurry, as if distorted. There were no shadows. As her steps took her past the falcon, it clearly moved its neck and followed her with its eyes until she had vanished.

"I sat on the sofa, completely confused. Then I started to cry. I don't know why. Finally, I reached behind my head and my hands touched her long scarf—the one she had worn around her neck. Mahlinja had left her scarf behind. I stared in amazement at the silky piece of cloth, twisted it again and again, crushed it in my fists, held it directly to my eyes, smelled it. The fabric was real. It was here. I hadn't been dreaming."

Adel fell silent. The story had troubled us both. I ordered a double whiskey and sipped it as I contemplated what he had told me. Finally, he asked me if I thought he was crazy. I replied no, and said that perhaps what he had described was an erotic dream. But he strongly denied this, pointing out that the sofa and his pubic hair were not damp, and there was no sperm at all.

"Where's the scarf today?" I asked.

"In a drawer in my bedroom," he said, smiling convincingly. "I can show it to you tomorrow. And don't forget the falcon. It was alive. And, as you will learn, it also played a role in the rest of my adventure."

"Well," I mused aloud, sipping my whiskey, "what happened next? How did you get back to the outside?"

By this time, it was midnight, and the waiter discreetly asked us to move to the bar so the staff could reset the tables for breakfast guests. We shuffled over with our glasses in hand and sat down in a dimly lit corner shielded by heavy, dark-red curtains and illuminated only by two candles. Once settled, Adel picked up the thread of his story.

HIDDEN TUNNELS

"I sat there confused," he said, "with Mahlinja's scarf between my fingers. I finally put the scarf around my neck, strode over to the wooden chair, and picked up my flashlight from the floor. Then I crossed to the stairs. As I turned to take a last look around the room, I saw the falcon fly gracefully to the chair with just three movements of its wings and land silently on top of the backrest. It looked directly at me.

"As I climbed back up the steps, I counted them. There were twenty-two. When I reached the burial chamber at the top, I looked again for the gap in the wall through which I had previously talked to my father. It was gone. On the floor, I found the bottles of water and the spare flashlight battery, so I knew I was in the right place. But I couldn't find the gap in the wall. I cried out for my father and the others—no answer. I nervously drank water from one of the bottles, then called out again, trying desperately to find a way out. But it was futile."

Adel looked at me, as if asking for my understanding.

"I was sixteen, he continued, just a boy with no archaeological experience and no way to tell how long I had been buried in this passage. I didn't know if it was day or night outside, whether the others had already returned with help. I knew something must have shifted again in the wall, because the gap no longer existed. Finally, I put one of the bottles of water in one bag and the battery in another, and went back down the stairs. The falcon was still perched on the back of the chair, and the yellow light was still glowing. Could I conjure up Mahlinja again? I lay down on the sofa, closed my eyes, and hoped for her to reappear. I called out her name, but to no avail. The falcon looked over at me, nodding as if he were omniscient.

"At some point, I fell asleep. When I woke up, I had no idea what time it was. I went back up the stairs to the burial chamber and called out again for the others. When I got no response, I began to consider other ways to find my way out of this underground prison. Could the falcon help me? After all, it had flown in from somewhere. And he needed food to survive. There had to be an opening. Shining my flashlight ahead of me, I once again climbed down the twenty-two stairs.

"The glowing stones continued to bathe the hall with their yellow light. The falcon was still perched on the back of the chair. I knelt directly in front of the bird and asked if it could speak. The bird stretched out his neck, but made no response. 'I have to get out of here,' I said, thinking it intensely at the same time. Then the falcon stretched its entire torso and, with just a few wing movements, flew over to the opposite wall, which was covered in hieroglyphs. It hovered there, rising and falling with the motion of its wings. Not understanding what it was trying to show me, I stood in front of the hieroglphs and asked the bird how to proceed. It turned its neck several times, but didn't seem to have understood me. 'Falcon, dear falcon,' I thought bravely, 'I can't decipher the characters. Please, please help me! In the name of Mahlinja, help me!' Moving its wings rapidly, almost like a hummingbird, the bird fluttered up and down the wall and touched some of the hieroglyphs with its beak.

"It was all so unreal. The glowing room, the black falcon, me in my jalabiya with Mahlinja's scarf around my neck. With its beak, the falcon kept touching certain characters and turning its neck to me. Then it returned to the back of the chair and stuck its head out toward me. Should I touch the characters? Which ones? In which order? 'Please, please, please dear falcon!' I cried. 'In the name of Mahlinja, show me again!' The bird then perched on my right shoulder like a trained parrot. I stood in front of the wall of hieroglyphs and every time the obviously intelligent animal touched a character, I tapped it with my finger.

"I touched eight characters in all. And as I learned years later, they were the characters of the eight most important gods in Egypt, including Osiris, Isis, Horus, and Amenti, who, in ancient Egypt, was the guardian of the entrance to the underworld. I had barely touched the eighth hieroglyph when I felt a gentle breeze that I hadn't noticed before. Until then, I had felt absolutely no air movement in the chamber. I went back to the wooden chair, the falcon perched peacefully on my right shoulder, and I reached for the flashlight. The yellow-lit walls still glowed, but now fresh air was coming in from somewhere. I moistened my fingers and stuck them up, trying to find the origin of the draft.

"I finally discovered a hole right under the sofa—one I hadn't seen before because the brocade cover reached to the floor. But the draft was definitely something new. Something must have opened somewhere. I laboriously pushed the sofa aside and shined my flashlight into a tunnel. As I began to climb down into it, the falcon flew off my shoulder and positioned himself again on the back of the chair.

"After descending a few steps, I came across side tunnels. Two ended abruptly—at least I couldn't go any further. A third led down at a slight angle but then was blocked by broken ceiling stones. But I could still feel the breeze, so I thought I might be on the right track. I shined my light into a fourth shaft that seemed to run straight and slightly downward, but I couldn't see the end of it."

At this point, Adel took a break and went to the restroom. We were still the only guests in the bar, so we told the waiter that he didn't have to wait around because of us. He didn't want to leave us alone, however, so I ordered a pot with strong black tea. It was apparently going to be a long night.

SAQQARA'S SECRETS

When Adel returned, I asked him if he could pinpoint the place under Saqqara where he had been. He drew a sketch on a paper napkin. "The grave wall that my father and his brother had opened and through which I crawled was only 400 meters away from the step pyramid," he said. "I have no idea of the location of the underground hall, however. I don't know whether it was to the left or the right of the step pyramid. But on one side, toward the Nile, there was a depression. So I should have been on the other side, under the pyramid."

I explained to Adel that, today, the field of ruins around the Saqqara pyramid is known to be teeming with underground tunnels that are several kilometers long. As an Egyptologist, Adel knew some of them and had led his tourist clients into similar tombs. But back in 1944, when Adel was sixteen, nobody knew about the mysterious world under Saqqara. Nor do we know everything about it today.

As early as 1728, French explorer Paul Lucas (1664–1737) reported on corridors under Saqqara. Then, in

November 1851, Auguste Mariette (1821–1881) discovered the phenomenal Serapeum, with tunnels under the desert sand that are wide enough to drive a tractor through. To the right and left of the main corridors, he found niches with the largest sarcophagi the world had ever seen (see color insert). Mariette had hoped to find the mummies of sacred Apis bulls in the sarcophagi. But the huge granite containers of the Serapeum were either empty or contained the cut-up bones of different animals.

Then beginning in 1964, British archaeologist Walter Bryan Emery (1903-1971) uncovered tomb after tomb under the floors of Saqqara, including mastabas from the Third Dynasty—around 5,000 years old. Finally, in the excavation season of 1968–1969, he discovered an "ark of animals" that included four million mummified ibis, 500,000 falcons, just as many baboons, and 200,000 crocodiles, along with eggs of the animals that were separately mummified. Emery came across curved main corridors from which over seventy side shafts branched off. These, in turn, split into more corridors, often on two levels and often parallel to each other.

Today, tourists can wander some of these tunnels and explore the tombs that lie under the desert sand of Saqqara—for example, the "Persian shaft," a system carved deep into the rock whose original purpose is puzzling. In fact, every tourist who wanders the ruins of Saqqara sooner or later stands in amazement in front of vertically driven shafts carved out of the rock, some as large as eight meters across (see Figures 18, 19, and 20).

Figures 18, 19, and 20. Tunnels and entrances to the underground in Sakkara.

No one—not even the experts—has a reasonable explanation for the mysterious tunnels under Saqqara (see color insert). We don't know when they were created, by whom, or why. So I was not surprised by Adel's story. But I knew that Saqqara is not the lost labyrinth, although the world beneath Saqqara is indeed labyrinthine (see Figures 21–24). After thinking about this, Adel returned to his story.

Figures 21 and 22. More tunnels and entrances to the underground in Sakkara.

"I didn't enter the tunnel right away," he said. "I remembered that the others were probably trying to get to me from the outside. So I left the glowing chamber for

Figures 23 and 24. More tunnels and entrances to the underground in Sakkara.

the third time, trudged up the twenty-two steps, and stood again in front of the wall through which I had originally crawled. There were still two full bottles of water on the floor. I drank one and listened for sounds from the outside. Where were the excavators pushing the granite blocks aside? Where were the men looking for me? Only after my rescue did I learn what had happened from my father.

"The chief archaeologists had completely prohibited the use of heavy equipment. The danger to any antiquities that might be destroyed was apparently more important to them than the life of a young boy. And they didn't want the public to know anything about the grave find— at least not until it had been evaluated archaeologically. Of course, my father and a few others continued to look for me. They managed to drill holes in several places and shouted my name, but received no answer.

"Despite the administration's ban on using heavy equipment, my father and his group of rescuers planned a night-time detonation, hoping to get me out and disappear quickly before the police came. If they were arrested for destroying antiquities, they would face prison sentences of several years. My life was aparently worth nothing compared to their antiquities. I don't know what the authorities were afraid of, but they would have let me starve and die of thirst."

UNANSWERED QUESTIONS

At this point, Adel broke off his narrative to express the frustration he felt over all the unanswered questions he

had. Because, in the end, the public never found out anything about the world hidden under Saqqara. And even
today, no journalist or archaeologist has asked questions
about the millions of mummified animals found—ibis,
falcons, baboons, crocodiles, dogs, fish, cats, snakes, rab-
bits, geese, even scorpions. Cattle embalmed, wrapped
with linen, and placed in canopic jars (ceramic vessels) or
wooden shrines, and the jars then placed into holes that
had to be punched into the walls. "Why doesn't anyone
care?" Adel wanted to know. "And where were the linen
fabrics produced? Where did the oil come from? How
many thousands of hands formed and baked the clay
pots? What was it all for?"

I shared Adel's rage as he asked these questions. In
fact, I had written about these issues several times. Quietly, without sounding like a know-it-all, I explained to
him what we know about the beliefs of the ancient Egyptians from pyramid texts, epitaphs, papyri, and the works
of ancient writers.

When the god Khnum created the first people, he
created them with two parts: the body (*khat*) and the
life force (*ka*). The khat is perishable; the ka is immor-
tal. The ancient Egyptians regarded the ka as part of the
great, universal spirit, the vibrations that animate everything. The body, on the other hand, is just a fleeting shell
that would have no life without the ka. The ka is spiritual,
omnipresent, and eternal.

In addition to these two parts, every life form also has
a *ba*, a state that only arises from the union of khat (flesh)

and ka (spirit). The ba can be seen as consciousness, as a psyche or mental force that only arises during a lifetime. When the body dies, the ka unites with the ba. In ancient Egypt, it was believed that the ka remained connected to the body even after death and that it was needed in order for the body to live on in the underworld. This belief led the Egyptians to the practice of mummifying bodies to preserve them for the afterlife.

In a sense, this idea contradicted their belief that the body was only worthless ballast that remained behind after the escape of the ka and the ba. The idea that the body also had to be preserved may have resulted from what ancient cultures knew about the coming destruction of the world, be it by water (flood) or fire from the sky (meteorites). The practice of mummification may have arisen from a belief in these ancient cultures that they would need to repopulate the Earth after these catastrophes.

By this time, it was 3 A.M. But neither Adel nor I thought of sleeping. The tea kept us awake. The waiter had dozed off peacefully behind the bar. We sat silently for a while, thinking. I wanted to know how Adel had escaped from the tunnels he had found. But he had other things on his mind.

"There's something rotten there," Adel whispered slowly. "If the ancients knew about a coming flood, why did they place their mummies underground? Surely they must have known that the waters from a flood would inundate all their underground facilities and destroy their mummies! There is something crucial that we haven't taken into account. And then there's the falcon! That bird was definitely alive. Can mummified falcons come to life? Do mummies have consciousness? Did they feel my presence?"

I had no answers to Adel's questions, but he kept pressing me.

"Where did Mahlinja come from? Nobody can tell me that she was a ghost or that I had an erotic dream. After all, I still have Mahlinja's scarf today. And how did she know my name? Why did she say she was waiting for me? For how long? And at what time? Can you tell me into what dimension my sperm disappeared? Am I the father of children somewhere in this crazy universe? In which era? In which location?"

I knew as little as Adel. I had read somewhere that there were states in quantum physics in which cause and effect were reversed. And then there are the theories about the simultaneity of the universe—that everything is happening *now*. There is no past and no future. And what about the idea that we humans are just characters in a kind of computer simulation that someone is playing somewhere in another dimension. These theories seem totally unreal to me—incomprehensible and incompatible with common sense.

"And there's something else," Adel added impatiently. "Ultimately, it is not just the mummified animals that puzzle me; it's also the tunnels themselves. How could the ancient Egyptians have cut fifty or more kilometers of tunnels out of solid rock? Iron and copper tools couldn't have done it; stone chisels couldn't have done it; and explosives did not exist at that time. From the time of the classical period of pharaohs, there is no evidence of tunnel construction on this gigantic scale. Planners, builders, and laborers worked on the surface. In fact, we more or less know which pharaohs commissioned these works. Grandiose temples were built; boulevards lined with hundreds of sphinxes were constructed; huge courtyards filled with columns were fashioned (see color insert). But these structures were all built on the surface, not deep underground. Of course, the pharaohs had their burial chambers broken out of the rock, but there is no mention of a huge tunnel system anywhere."

Adel gave me a challenging look and pressed on. "And why did they set up their temples on the surface when they knew that the Earth was in for catastrophic events? When generations of people were convinced of a coming flood that would destroy all their incomparable buildings? You said that the world of mummies was created so that the planet could be filled with life again after the destruction. But this belief runs counter to the construction of magnificent buildings on the surface. So this underground world of tunnels must be thousands of years older than the structures they built on the surface."

Adel looked at me intently. "And I know this underground world exists, because I walked about five kilometers of it myself. And definitely not in the same rooms that Emery discovered over twenty years later."

But I had no more answers for Adel and I encouraged him to return to his story.

THE GEMSTONE PATH

"Having discovered these tunnels," he went on, "I was faced with the decision of whether to enter them in hopes of finding another exit. I decided to trust the falcon and returned to the glowing chamber. After a few moments of hesitation, I bravely stepped into the shaft.

"The tunnel seemed endless. I estimate I walked a good half hour before the light from my flashlight gave out. I was getting hungry and thirsty, so I drank the last bottle of water and replaced the battery. Then I started to wonder what I would do when that last battery gave out. So I slowly turned around and returned to the now-familiar glowing chamber. As soon as I crawled out of the hole under the sofa, the falcon perched on my right shoulder, as if it had expected me. I sat down on the sofa and thought: 'Falcon, how do I get back to the light?' The animal flew a meter in the air, dropped down again, and landed on the floor in front of me with both claws at the same time. This happened four times. Finally, I thought intensely and said out loud: 'Falcon, I don't understand.' The black bird tilted its neck, then spread its wings and jumped about two meters in the air, immediately landing back on the floor with both claws at the same time.

"Not sure that I understood, I started to imitate the bird, making wing movements with my arms and elbows, hopping up off the floor, and stomping my feet as I landed. And then my eyes caught what looked like a tiny red dot about ten meters in front of me on the floor. I went to the spot and bent down. A tiny gemstone glowed there. I pried it out. It wasn't much bigger than my thumbnail, and it wasn't yellow like the stones in the walls. It was a dark ruby red.

"My admiration for the falcon grew immeasurably. Like the falconers of old, I offered him my forearm. He immediately perched on it as if we were a well-rehearsed team. Then I looked him straight in the eye and asked: 'Falcon, who are you?' The bird merely nodded in response. When I repeated my question, he made some neck movements that reminded me of the letter 'S' and the name Sisi came to my mind spontaneously. 'I'll call you Sisi,' I whispered to him. Then I thought: 'Thank you for your help.' When I got up, Sisi fluttered to the back of the chair.

"I crawled back into the hole under the sofa. Tunnels always lead from one place to another, I told myself, and I bravely walked into the unknown. Every a few meters, I hopped or stomped on the stone floor, causing it to vibrate. Each time I did this, a dark red light began to glow, sometimes as far as 200 meters ahead of me. It was about the size of a firefly, but bright enough so that I could see the course of the tunnel. I don't know how long I walked. Years later, in the Egyptian army, I learned that, with normal strides, a man can walk around four kilometers an hour. I estimate that I traveled more than an hour in total. The tunnel walls, by the way, felt smooth, as if they had been milled, but they did not contain any inscriptions."

When Adel paused, I asked him if he was getting tired. It was after 4:00 A.M. and I was worried about him. I told him I would ask for a room for him at the hotel, but he refused. He wanted to finish his story. He said he wanted to get some fresh air, and that he would be back soon. While he was gone, I picked up my voice recorder and retold the most important parts of his story on tape.

Half an hour later, Adel returned. He said that he had called his wife so that she wouldn't be worried about his absence. He wanted to know if I was "on my last leg yet." I said I felt fine. The clanking of dishes in the restaurant next to the bar, and the chattering of voices of the first breakfast groups and early risers who had to leave for the airport began to fill the room. Our exhausted waiter was finally relieved, but not before we rewarded him generously. Before Adel began again, I pointed to my tape recorder. He had no objection and picked up the story where he had left off.

GUARDIAN THRONES

"I couldn't take the falcon into the tunnel with me," he recalled, "because the shaft was too narrow to carry a bird weighing several kilos on my shoulders, so Sisi stayed in the hall. After about an hour, I suddenly saw two dark-red dots glowing side by side in the side wall of the tunnel.

To the left of that light, I discovered a well shaft. Thanks to the flashlight, I found some steps that led me down to what tasted like cool and fresh groundwater. It dawned on me that even the builders of the tunnel couldn't have managed without water. After refreshing myself, I filled my own empty bottle. Then I marched on for another half hour. I was very hungry, but I could deal with that. At least now I had water.

"At some point, the dark-red lights disappeared. I stomped my feet, hopped up and down, and shouted as loudly as I could to cause a vibration, but no lights appeared. As I shined the beam of my flashlight around me, I discovered that I was now in a large room about twenty meters square whose walls were covered with hieroglyphs. I saw a throne that stood on a kind of dais, not on the floor. Seven steps led up to it. I was awestruck because the throne in front of me blazed with glittering gold. Nobody was seated on it. There were no stones glowing in the walls as in the other chamber, so my flashlight could only illuminate small portions of the room at a time. When I pounded on a wall with my fists, colored characters loosened, splintered, and fell to the floor.

"To the right and left of the first step to the throne were the figures of two lions, their mouths grimly open. On the ceiling directly above the throne was a kind of matt, shiny hemisphere. The walls were covered with hieroglyphs and adorned with statues of various gods. I was overcome with awe and fear."

Adel stopped for a second and asked a waiter for a glass of chilled orange juice and some toast with butter and honey. I ordered the same. Then he continued.

"As before, the ceiling showed a dark-blue starry sky across which elaborate barges sailed [see color insert]. I saw Horus and his winged sun discs. And directly above the throne, a huge eagle spread its wings. When I respectfully approached the bottom step and put my foot on it, I felt a weak electric shock—just strong enough to make me stand still. Even years later, I have wondered where that electricity came from. From what source did that energy emanate? I still had the protective cloth over my jalabiya to protect myself against possible toxins, and I still had Mahlinja's scarf. So I rolled up the sturdy cotton cloth and threw it on the steps as protection against the electrical charge. In the light of my flashlight, I saw one of the idols move with amazing speed. Then my cotton cloth flew through the air and landed to the side of the throne's dais. Heaven only knows what spirits were present there, but I understood that climbing those steps could be deadly, so I refrained from it."

Here I interrupted Adel. "Do the words *Targum Scheni* mean anything to you?" I asked. When he shook his head no, I explained.

"*Targum* is the Hebrew word for 'explanation,' I told him. "The *Targum Scheni* is a portion of the *Book of Ester* that describes King Solomon's throne, which was just as dangerous as the one that you discovered. This work, which goes back thousands of years, describes Solomon's throne as a miracle that was created by spirits.[1] It was unique and was made solely for his use. Beside the throne, a total of seventy-two golden lions and seventy-two golden eagles faced each other, each eagle's right foot facing a lion's left foot."

Adel interrupted hastily. "That hall must have been much larger than the throne room in which I found myself. Seventy-two lions and seventy-two eagles would never have fit in there."

"Keep listening," I said, smiling. "It gets even more amazing." And I went on to further describe the strange throne.

In the upper part of the back of the throne was a round dome made of matt shimmering material similar to the hemisphere he had described, I told Adel. This apparently acted as a kind of switch that activated a series of mechanical protectors. To get to the throne, visitors had to walk up six metal steps, each watched over by a protective mechanism. The first was guarded by a bull and a lion; the second by a bear and a lamb; the third by a bear and an anka, a type of cat; the fourth by an eagle and a peacock; the fifth by a cat and a rooster; and the sixth by a hawk and a pigeon. There were also twenty-one mechanical wings moving on the ceiling that provided King Solomon with air and shade.

Whenever Solomon wished to ascend his throne, these mechanical guardians were set in motion. From the first step, the lion raised him to the second; from the second, the bear raised him to the third; and so on up to the sixth step. When others tried to approach the king, however, the bull mooed, the lion roared, the bear growled, the sheep bleated, the cat meowed, the peacock screeched, the rooster crowed, the hawk screamed, and the pigeons chirped.

After Solomon's death, the Babylonian king Nebuchadnezzar tried to ascend the mysterious throne, but the mechanical lion dislocated his left hip and the bear smashed his right. Decades later, Alexander of Macedonia captured the throne and had it shipped to Egypt. But when Sisak, the king of Egypt, tried to ascend the throne, the lion broke his right hip on the first step. Sisak fled from the throne and has been called the "limping pharaoh" ever since.

"You see, Adel," I said, "mechanical robots existed even in the remote past. So the throne you stood before does not seem an impossibility to me."

As the first rays of sunlight appeared in the sky, Adel and I took turns walking over to the breakfast buffet. We were both so energized by all that we had shared that night that we still didn't feel tired. "Don't stop now," I said. "How did you finally see daylight again?" Adel settled back and continued his tale.

MYSTERIOUS MAPS

"The throne room was dark," he recalled. "The only light came from my flashlight, so my perspective remained very limited. There were two gilded chests set against one wall, but I couldn't lift their lids. In fact, during my whole adventure in that subterranean world, I wasn't able to open a single container. On the wall across from the throne, I saw a confusing depiction that did not seem to match the style of the hieroglyphs. It was a relief with curved lines, set with small precious stones at various points and depicting something like a ship between the lines. Not a sailing ship as we know it, but clearly a hull with an unknown structure. I couldn't make heads or tails of it, although I tried illuminating it from different angles.

"Ultimately, it dawned on me that it had to be a map. But of what? I was familiar with the contours of the Mediterranean and the world beyond and realized that I was probably looking at a map of the world rather than a map of a country. But at sixteen, I lacked the insight to realize that, in ancient Egypt, such a world map simply *couldn't* have existed. The pharaohs knew nothing about the coastlines beyond Gibraltar. They didn't know of North, or Central, or South America. Yet there, in front of my eyes, on the wall opposite the throne and lit by my own flashlight, was what was undoubtedly a multicolored relief of a map of the world."

"Do you have an explanation for that?" he challenged me. Actually, I did.

In my book *Chariots of the Gods*, I had written about the old maps of a Turkish admiral named Piri Reis.[2] On November 9, 1929, Halil Eldem, then director of the Topkapi Palace in Istanbul, found two map fragments. They were painted in delicate colors on gazelle skin and were clearly the work of Piri Reis, who had served in the Turkish Navy 400 years earlier (see Figure 25).

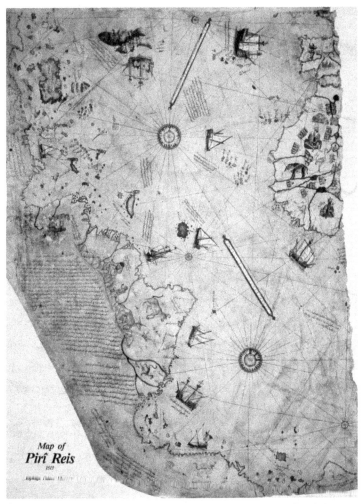

Figure 25. The map drawn by admiral Piri Reis in the Topkapi Palace in Istanbul, Turkey. (Charles H. Hapgood, New York, 1966)

But Piri Reis not only drafted various maps, he also wrote about them. In a work entitled *Bahriye*, he noted:

> *These [the maps] have been drawn by poor Piri Reis, son of Haji Mehmet, who is known as the nephew of Kemal Reis, in the city of Gelibolu. God forgive them both, in the month of the Most Holy Muharrem, in the year 919 [March 9, 1513].*

In 1954, copies of this map were given to American cartographer Arlington H. Mallery, who was known among experts as a specialist in old nautical charts. Mallery was intrigued by the fragments because they featured continents like Antarctica and parts of South America that had not yet been discovered in 1513 when Piri Reis lived. Piri Reis noted in his writings that he had constructed his own map from twenty different maps. "Nobody owns a map like that at this time," he wrote.

Mallery asked a colleague from the U. S. Hydrographic Institute for help in his analysis. The accuracy of the distances shown between the Old and the New World startled them both right away. After all, in 1513, America was not marked on any map. The two cartographers also quickly noticed that Piri Reis had not used the coordinates commonly employed at that time, which showed the Earth as a flat disk. To get to the bottom of this riddle, the researchers transferred the old map to a modern grid that represented the Earth as spherical rather than flat. To their surprise, they found that, not only were the contours of North and South America accurately drawn, but also the coastline of Antarctica (see Figure 26).

Figure 26. Scheme of the Piri Reis map. (Charles H. Hapgood, New York, 1966)

On the Piri Reis map, the tip of South America from Tierra del Fuego runs in a narrow land connection to the south and then spreads out toward Antarctica. Today, a stormy sea rages south of Tierra del Fuego. The Piri Reis map was compared millimeter by millimeter with sea-floor profiles that had been produced using the most modern means—sonar and radiation sensors. This analysis clearly established that there was a land connection between Tierra del Fuego and Antarctica some 11,000 years ago.

Today, this land bridge lies under a thick sheet of ice. In 1957, W. M. Lineham, a Jesuit priest who was then director of the Weston Observatory in Connecticut, examined the old maps, along with Capt. Mallery. They concluded that the Piri Reis map was incredibly precise, especially as far as Antarctica was concerned. On August 28, 1958, they attended a conference led by Peter Warren at Georgetown University.

Here are statements from the minutes:

Warren noted that it is difficult for us today to understand how cartographers could be so precise so many centuries ago, when we have only recently begun using modern scientific methods in cartography. Mallery concurred, arguing that such a precise map could not have been drawn without an airplane. Yet the fact is that the longitudes on these maps are absolutely correct, something that we were only able to do two centuries ago.

With the seismic method, Lineham added, we are finding things that confirm many of the drawings made on the Piri Reis map, including land masses, mountains, and even islands hidden below the ice. It seems, in fact, that this map is more accurate than we were inclined to believe.

When Charles H. Hapgood, often called the "doyen of cartography," examined the Piri Reis map he concluded:

The Antarctic coastlines must have been mapped before they were covered in ice. The ice in this area is about 1 mile thick today. We have no idea how the data on this map can be reconciled with the geographic knowledge of 1513.[3]

This clearly demonstrates that anthropologists, archaeologists, and pre-historians of all stripes have been pussyfooting around this topic and won't acknowledge what can be clearly proven.

After I explained about the Piri Reis map, Adel seemed to be overwhelmed and remarked angrily that these things should be taught at universities.

"Well, it get's even crazier," I warned.

King Solomon, Suleiman in the Arab world, used world maps like this thousands of years ago. They were indispensable to him, because he had several flying devices, and you can't fly around the world without maps. These flying machines are described in the Ethiopian royal book, the so-called *Kebra Nagast*.[4] There, the "Carriage of the Skies" is described in detail and, in chapter 58, even its speed is given. Egyptian geographer and historian Al-Masudi (c. 895–956 AD) spoke of these machines as well. Called "Herodotus of Arabia" by some scholars, Al-Masudi reports that Solomon had maps that showed the Earth with its continents and seas, including both the inhabited and uninhabited areas, and even showing their plants and animals, "and many other, extremely amazing things."[5]

For the first time, Adel was speechless. He shook his head and pounded the table with his palms. "This is just insane!" he exploded. "Why is nobody writing about this?"

"I did write about it," I replied. [6] "It just doesn't seem to interest anyone. But let's get back to your story. I still don't know how you came to see daylight again."

Confused, Adel shook his head. Then he grumbled while he smeared some butter and honey on his toast and continued.

BACK TO THE LIGHT

"There was nowhere in the room to sit except on the throne," Adel pointed out, "and that was dangerous. So I walked around the walls, gently pressing on them with my thighs and elbows hoping to find an opening. After all, people had built the hall and they had to get their tools and equipment in there somehow—and probably not through the kilometer-long corridor that lay behind me. I had little desire to walk all the way back. So, out of anger and despair, I punched a spot on the wall that was covered with hieroglyphs. They all shattered and feel to the ground as if they were made of plaster, and an opening appeared that was just wide enough for my torso. So I crawled in, gripping my flashlight firmly and wondering how long my battery would last.

"The shaft led upward at an angle to a few steps and another bend. And suddenly it seemed to me as if I heard voices from afar. I hardly dared to breathe. There were definitely voices in front of me, although weak. I crept to the point where the jumble of voices seemed the loudest, and I shouted with all my strength: 'Help! Help! Help!' I kept shouting and waiting and hoping for an answer. I finally heard a deep male baritone voice as if through a filter: 'Where are you? Who are you?' I shouted back that I was trapped in a crypt but that I could hear the person speaking. Then the voice fell silent.

"After a few minutes, the voice asked if there was a rocky ledge or a bend in the crypt that I could hide behind. I called back: 'Why?' The voice answered that they wanted to detonate a small explosive charge, but that they could only do that if I could protect myself. I described my situation and the voice told me to stand behind the ledge and press my cloth over my head. So I stepped back and waited.

"After a few minutes, I felt an explosion followed by a short, intense rush of air. I crawled forward on all fours and saw bright daylight beyond the bend. Several men stood outside staring at me as if I were a ghost. They asked my name and wanted to know how I had gotten into the tunnel. One of the men knew my father and exclaimed excitedly: 'This is Adel, the missing boy from Saqqara!' The men handed me flat bread, dates, melon slices, and fresh drinking water. I crouched on a stone, covered my eyes from the sunlight, and cried. When I asked where I was, someone told me I was in Memphis, a good five kilometers from Saqqara.

"I later learned that the Temple of Ptah in Memphis is said to have been built in prehistoric times by Menes and that the word 'Memphis' originally meant 'white wall.' Memphis became the first capital of the Old Kingdom. Countless coronation ceremonies were held there, hence the throne room I had found. Later, anyone who thought of himself as important wanted to be buried near Memphis.

"The men who found me turned out to be road builders. That's why they had explosives. At that time, there was no telephone connection to my parents' home, so the foreman drove me home in his car. You cannot imagine everybody's joy when I arrived. At first, they thought I had returned from the spirit world. My mother wouldn't stop crying, and everyone praised Allah and kissed me almost continuously. My father called his friends together, as well as his brother and my cousin.

"In the days that followed, I was passed around from one person to the next. A daily newspaper even printed a picture of me. And I had to tell my story over and over. But I didn't reveal everything. I kept silent about my intimate encounter with Mahlinja. When my mother asked me where I had gotten the scarf, I didn't lie. I just said that a beautiful girl had put it around my neck."

"And now, my friend," Adel said, leaning back in his chair, "I'm starting to feel weak. We should allow ourselves a few hours of sleep."

"Just one more thing," I said and took his hand. "What happened to the grave that your father and his brother opened and through which you entered?"

"The grave is shown to selected tourists today. It is referred to as the 'family grave of a rich vizier.' The passage that led to the twenty-two steps was sealed off."

Adel began to put on his jacket, but I stopped him. "Did you ever see the falcon again?"

Laughing, Adel sat back down, resigned to tell the final chapter in his story.

SISI'S RETURN

"Half a year after my rescue," he said, "I was a passenger on a small truck that was transporting wheelbarrows and tools for a Czech archaeological team working in Saqqara. I was helping with the unloading when I saw a falcon circling above our heads. It seemed to me that is was cawing wearily.

"I looked up, called out the name Sisi several times, and raised my right forearm. The falcon immediately came down and perched on it. Now I can't tell one falcon from another, but the one that perched on my forearm nodded continuously and rubbed his head on my upper arm. The older workers asked if I had trained it. Then the falcon hopped from my forearm onto my right shoulder. The bird seemed old and tired and, when the workers started moving again, the falcon clung to the side of the truck as we drove off. A few minutes later, he tipped over and fell off. The others wanted to leave him there, but I convinced them to let me wrap the bird in my towel and bring it home.

"My father, who knew the story of Sisi, stroked the bird's body and asked: 'What are you going to do?'

"Without thinking, I said: 'Embalm him.' Someone in our family of doctors knew a conservator—those who prepared mummies for the museums. After some negotiations, my father convinced him that Sisi was my personal falcon and that I wanted to keep him at home without him decaying. The procedure took eight weeks, but when I got Sisi back, he looked alive.

"Months later, I managed to get an old canopic jar and put Sisi in it. I sealed it with resin and, with my father's help, took it to Tuna el-Gebel, where, a year earlier, an underground necropolis with falcon and baboon mummies had been discovered. Each mummy was in its own jar and each jar was placed in its own recess in the wall. There weren't millions of mummies there as were found in Saqqara twenty-five years later; there were only about a hundred.

"Before we walked stooped-fashion into the underground crypt, I hid the jar containing Sisi in my shoulder bag. At that time, the Tuna el-Gebel system had no electric lights. So while my father smoked a cigarette with the guard outside, I used my flashlight to locate an empty recess in the dark wall and put Sisi into it, amidst other jars filled with falcon mummies. Sisi has been resting there ever since, among his kind and hopefully for millennia. Or perhaps, until the day when he will materialize again."

CHAPTER 5

Paradigm Shift

THE WAY WE MARK TIME IS RELATIVE. According to the Christian calendar, we live in the year 2020 as this book is being written. We are in the third millennium. By contrast, the Jewish community is currently living in Shabbat 5, Sivan 5780—the sixth millennium—because their calendar began as early as 3761 BC. The Muslim calendar, on the other hand, began in 622 AD—or 1398, according to the Christian calendar. To make things even more confusing, the Mayan calendar started on August 11, 3114 BC, which, according to the Christian calendar, would be the year 5134 BC.

In fact, every culture has its own calendar, and the starting point for each one has always been an important event described in a holy book or historical record. For

Christians, it is marked by the birth of Jesus as described in the Gospels. For Jews, it is marked by the creation of the world as described in the Old Testament. For Muslims, it is marked by the entrance of the Prophet into Medina as told in the Koran. For the Maya in distant Central America, it is marked by the visit of extraterrestrials as told in a book called *Jaguar Priests,* one of the *Chilam Balam* books written four centuries ago in Yucatec Maya, the language of the Mayan tribes.

> *Back then they descended from the road of the stars. They spoke the magical language of the stars of the heavens. Yes, their sign gives us certainty that they came from heaven. And when they descend again, the thirteen gods and the nine gods, they will put in order again what they once created.*[1]

And I believe that they have indeed descended again. They are currently orbiting our planet, studying our languages, learning about our political and religious relationships, cataloging our weapon systems, and exploring our knowledge of viruses and bacteria. And although this has rarely, if ever, been reported, I believe that we are currently caught up in the vortex of a paradigm shift. The zeitgeist is changing.

First reports started leaking out in September 2017 in a story called "Wonders of the Cosmos" that appeared in the popular American science magazine *Scientific American.* The article sought to familiarize readers gently with the possibility that there was, in fact, life out there.[2] Then, on October 20, 2017, the American weekly magazine *Time* followed up with a special edition whose cover asked the question: "Are We Alone?" The answer was clear: No, we are not.[3] Just days later, *Newsweek* released an article entitled "Life Beyond Earth?"[4] And in March 2019, the world-famous magazine *National Geographic* began a whole series on the topic of extraterrestrial life. But by then, the question mark was gone and the story was titled unequivocally "We Are Not Alone."[5] In Germany, *P. M. Magazine* approached the hot topic with a cover story titled "Ready For Contact."[6] And in Switzerland, the prestigious *Neue Zürcher Zeitung* devoted an entire issue to the question: "Who Is Out There?"[7]

But these are just a few of the hundreds of magazines published worldwide. It is rather the programming of powerful broadcast TV outlets that appears to be turning the tide toward a serious discussion of these questions. In the United States, the History Channel has been broadcasting a series entitled *Ancient Aliens* for over ten years, with three sequels originally planned. Over 160 episodes have already been produced and another forty are in production. TV series like *The X Files* have been very successful as well, and many documentaries have been produced in many languages for broadcast worldwide. The large, multilingual Internet broadcaster GAIA, which is accessed worldwide, ran a forty-part series on extraterrestrials that was a resounding success, while the so-called AlienCon, a convention that explores the topic of extraterrestrials, takes place in the United States each year, drawing large crowds. Around 20,000 people attended

AlienCon in Los Angeles in June 2019. The spirit of the times has indeed changed.

VISITORS FROM THE SKIES

On May 26, 2019, the *New York Times* shocked its readers with the headline: "Wow—What Is That? Navy Pilots Report Unexplained Flying Objects." Their astonished readers learned that, from summer 2014 to March 2015, several Navy pilots had observed unidentifiable foreign objects on their radar screens at high altitude. They chased them with their fighter jets and also filmed them. These impressive images were released by the Defense Department and can be downloaded from the Internet, along with the conversations recorded between the pilots.[8]

Lieutenant Danny Accoin, one of the pilots who talked to the *Times*, reported that, in the summer of 2014, he was part of Fighter Squadron VFA-11, known as the "Red Rippers," operating from the aircraft carrier USS Theodore Roosevelt. He and a fellow pilot, Lieutenant Graves, flew over the Virginia coast in fighter jets equipped with the most advanced radar systems. They first encountered the foreign objects at an altitude of 10,000 meters and later spotted them again, flying and changing their positions at incredible speeds. The objects performed maneuvers that no earthly technology would allow and that no human pilot could carry out.

Lieutenant Accoin captured images of the eerie objects twice—first on his radar, and then on both his radar and his onboard infrared camera. Whatever it was, it was real. It was definitely radiating heat. Lieutenant Graves described the experience to the *Times* reporter:

> *Our exercises are complex maneuvers, in which we climb to 10,000 meters and then dive down. The [foreign] objects can accelerate, decelerate and then take off again at a supersonic speed.*[9]

Of course, the pilots discussed the sightings with each other and wondered whether the alleged UFOs might be drones from a secret U. S. Air Force program. But that thought was quickly dropped when a squadron pilot "in total shock" came back from a mission and said he almost crashed into one of the objects.

Two other pilots were flying side by side at a distance of around 100 meters when suddenly a cube-like object with a sphere in the middle pushed between them and maneuvered at the same speed as the two pilots. They were so frightened that they asked for the flight to be abandoned immediately and later filed a report about the incident.

All of the pilots involved testified that the eerie objects were able to accelerate rapidly from zero to supersonic speed, stop suddenly in the air, and make right-angled U-turns—something that was impossible with any current aeronautic technology. Not even drones can do that.[10]

Startled by these reports, several politicians made inquiries to the Defense Department asking if the reports were correct and if national security was at risk. The deputy chairman of the Senate Intelligence Committee gave this statement out to journalists: "If naval pilots experience inexplicable disturbances in the air, then it is a security issue that . . . we need to look into carefully."[11]

The stunned senators learned in incremental steps that pilots of the F/A-18 fighter jets from the aircraft carrier Nimitz had already reported UFO sightings in 2004, ten years before those reported by the *New York Times*. The 2019 *Times* article reporting the pilot's observations had barely hit the streets when the skeptics started commenting. In an objective article in the *Washington Post*, Professor Daniel Drezner put the situation into perspective—but did not rule out extraterrestrials.[12] On the other hand, in Germany, a *Der Spiegel* headline mockingly announced: "911 from Outer Space." But the article's author, Marco Evers, still wasn't convinced. "Researchers have now discovered thousands of planets in other solar systems," he explained, "but there is still no evidence of the existence of even an extraterrestrial microbe." *Der Spiegel* dismissed the UFO believers as fringe elements in American pop culture, and the reports as Hollywood fictions or children's fantasies. According to them, "all alleged alien flying objects can be explained satisfactorily. Sometimes they were weather balloons, sometimes birds, meteorites, ice crystals, or illusions; forgeries have also been detected."[13]

True, and yet not true.

It is true that there have always been false and even fraudulent claims of UFO sightings. And it is also true that there are natural explanations for countless UFO sightings. But how many sightings have there been?

To find out, Linda Miller, a psychologist at the University of Maryland, teamed up with Cheryl Costa, a journalist who had been writing objectively about UFOs in various newspapers for years. Over a period of eight years, the two women studied only those UFO reports that had been received by government agencies. The result was a 360-page report full of tables that showed that, between 2001 and 2015, a total of 121,036 UFO sightings were registered with the U. S. authorities.[14] Experience shows, however, that, after witnessing an unusual spectacle of lights in the sky, only about one tenth of all witnesses report these events to any agency. So that means that perhaps as many as 1,210,036 UFO sightings have occurred over those fifteen years.

A survey by *National Geographic Magazine* found that 36 percent of Americans strongly believe in UFOs and 47 percent think UFOs are likely real. Moreover, 70 percent of all Americans believe that the authorities have not given them correct information about UFO activity. The population of the United States is currently around 330 million people. That means that some 230 million Americans don't trust the government authorities when it comes to UFOs. At the end of their report, Costa and Miller write: "The UFOs are not just about lights in the sky, but about real lies on Earth."

TRUE BELIEVERS

It is becoming more and more clear that UFO skeptics are the "true believers" here—the ones unable to separate facts from ideology. They don't check anything, and they don't want to take the arguments of others into account. They believe stubbornly and confidently that there simply are no extraterrestrials or UFOs. Moreover, anyone who tries to defend the reality of UFOs against them is simply labeled "stupid."[15] Serious people don't believe in UFOs. End of story! And the few educated and courageous people who try to discuss the topic end up in the garbage heap of ridicule. TV programs like *The Truth about UFOs* show spectacular UFO sightings, only to have them refuted during the same broadcast by pseudo-eggheads.[16] The message is always the same: UFO witnesses are whackos—all of them. The anti-UFO lobby always wins, even if its arguments are unspeakable nonsense.

Skeptics claim that no one has ever presented objective evidence for UFOs. When clear photographs or even films are provided as evidence of an extraordinary experience, they are simply dismissed as hoaxes by so-called experts who wag their fingers sagely. When hundreds or even thousands of people describe the same UFO event, they are dismissed as victims of "mass suggestion" or even "mass hysteria." They observed a "mirage" or "parts of rockets or space stations" that crash all over the world, 365 days a year, in an apparent never-ending bombardment of earthly garbage from space. Or the supposed UFOs are claimed to be light-weight airplanes, or children's kites, or hot-air balloons, or reflections of spotlights, or hallucinations, inventions, and fantasies, or swarms of mosquitoes, or weather balloons, or ice crystals, or swamp gas, or brilliant planets or meteors that were just circling the Earth at night at incredible speeds. Just about any explanation will do, as long as it's not UFOs.

The anti-UFO lobby always cloaks its arguments in serious language and uses disparagement and exclusion to assert the "scientific character" of its conclusions. These pseudo-scientists are completely convinced that any research into UFOs is, by definition, spurious simply because there *are* no UFOs. In religion and ideology, that is referred to as "belief"; in depth psychology, it's called "repression."

When will these true believers finally acknowledge that they are flying in the face of facts? On June 25, 1965, the then British Minister of Defense told staff: "Our policy is to downplay the subject of UFOs and to avoid attaching undue attention or publicity to it."[17] The U. S. Central Intelligence Agency issued the following directive over sixty years ago:

> *All authorities in the secret service network are required to influence the mass media for the purpose of discrediting and to infiltrate civilian UFO research groups . . . UFO reports must be criticized as untrustworthy and ridiculed . . . public interest in UFO incidents is to be undermined.*[18]

This explosive order, made public only in 1975 through the so-called Robertson Panel Report, should be enough to convince even the most stubborn UFO skeptics that, for decades, they have been abused as useful idiots. Countless responsible people have now understood this, as I show in a recent book, among them Denis Letty, Major General of the French Air Force; Ricardo Bermúdez Sanhueza, General of the Chilean Air Force; José Carlos Pereira, Commander in Chief of the Brazilian Air Force; Fife Symington, Governor of Arizona; Yves Sillard, former Director General of the French Space Agency; Paul Theodore Hellyer, former Minister of Defense of Canada; Professor John Mack of Harvard University; and American astronaut Edgar Dean Mitchell.[19] Without exception, each of these individuals confirms the existence of flying objects that use non-terrestrial technology.

All idiots? Irresponsible individuals? "Big kids" and "nonsense," as *Der Spiegel* claimed? When will members of the anti-UFO community realize that it is *they* who are deluded? It is *they* who don't want to admit that some people may already carry implants from extraterrestrials? Some of these implants have been surgically removed and thoroughly analyzed—physically and chemically. They are verifiable scientifically for anyone who wants to know.[20]

RENDLESHAM FOREST

One single example is enough to show the weakness of the skeptics' arguments. On December 26, 1980, at the

Royal Air Force base at Bentwaters-Woodbridge, England, an irrefutable sighting occurred. At the time, twenty-five-year-old James Penniston had been assigned to the RAF's tactical squad as a security officer. Shortly after midnight, Sergeant Steffens informed him that lights had been sighted in nearby Rendlesham Forest. It was not a crashed plane; something had landed there. Penniston immediately informed the base's control center and ordered two guards, Edward Cabansag and John Burroughs, to accompany him to investigate. In the forest, they observed a glaring light. As they approached, they saw the clear outline of a triangular object that stood on three legs in a forest clearing. As they approached, they saw blue and yellow sparks swarming around the strange object.

At the same time, their radio communication with the base was cut off. The air was alive with an electrical charge. The men felt it on their uniforms, on their skin, and in their hair, describing it later as akin to a static charge. Penniston told Cabansag to walk back to a position where he could reestablish contact with the base. Then he and Burroughs slowly circled the glowing object. Penniston took several pictures and decided that the object could only be an aircraft. Then he noticed several foreign symbols on one side that were "three inches high and two and a half feet wide" and did not correspond to any earthly alphabet.[21]

After about ten minutes of observation, Penniston dared to touch the object. The surface felt smooth and warm. After about twenty-five minutes, the object began to glow more strongly and the men took cover. Without a sound, the object lifted off the ground, maneuvered through the trees, and darted off over the tree tops at an incredible speed. After daybreak, the men returned to the forest clearing and found some broken branches on the ground, which they concluded had been knocked there by the strange object. In the frozen ground, they also discovered three deep indentations, as well as burn marks on several trees.

Colonel Charles Halt served as deputy commander of Bentwaters RAF base at that time. The next day, he visited the landing site of the strange object with other members of the RAF teams. They recorded the three imprints in the ground and measured them. Each was thirty-five centimeters in diameter and four centimeters deep, and together they formed an isosceles triangle. The radioactivity level measured was above average, so the the men decided to leave the uncanny place quickly. James Penniston died of an inexplicable blood disorder a few years later. Colonel Charles Halt resigned from the RAF in 1991 and served as Inspector General of the Ministry of Defense. He is completely convinced that the foreign object was controlled by an intelligence. But was it a human intelligence?

Definitely not.

And there's more. The base radar at Bentwaters had registered the flying object on the screen. Its measured speed as it left Rendlesham Forest was over 6,500 kilometers per hour. This caused it to appear on the radar screen as a continuous line rather than the usual flashing dots.

Moreover, the object disappeared vertically into space, not horizontally somewhere behind the trees. Penniston repeatedly asserted that the technology of that aircraft was far beyond anything that man could control.

What do the skeptics say? That Penniston and his people were victims of an optical illusion. They had been irritated by the light from the Orford Ness Lighthouse, which is about one mile away. The lights could also have come from swamp gases, skeptics suggested. Or if it was, in fact, an object, it was probably a secret drone—as if in 1980, forty years ago, drones that could have performed in this way even existed. As if the lights of a lighthouse could press four centimeters deep into frozen ground, leave burn marks on trees, and separate branches from their trunks. Only a complete fool would believe such nonsense.

Even by 2014, when Accoin and Graves reported their sightings, there were no drones of earthly origin that could fly at an altitude of 10,000 meters, accelerate rapidly from zero to supersonic speeds, and perform right-angled maneuvers. There were no drones that could slip between two fighter jets and fly along with them. No drones that, as in the Bentwaters case, contained unearthly symbols. At some point, they will have to abandon these foolish explanations.

MESSAGES FROM THE SKIES

In 1959, NASA had already commissioned a report on UFOs from the Brooking Committee, an American think tank made up of experts of the highest caliber.[22] The resulting report deals with the question of how to prepare mankind for contact with extraterrestrials. Even back then, sixty years ago, scientists recommended that the human community should be informed in small increments about the existence of extraterrestrials. Headlines like "Extraterrestrials Are Here" or "We Are Being Watched by Extraterrestrials," they said, would be too disruptive for human society to absorb. Religious and political systems might collapse. But is that necessarily true?

On June 13, 2019, a huge formation appeared in a cornfield near the village of Saint-Hippolyte, not far from Colmar in Alsace, France. The farmer who owned the field, Thomas Jehl, was taken completely by surprise and could not explain the formation, which consisted of several circles of different sizes.

An IT specialist named Patrick Wenger lived not far from Saint-Hippolyte. He was a practical man with both feet planted firmly on the ground; he was also a trained drone pilot. Wenger sent his drone over the formation and provided me with some impressive photos (see color insert). He also strode across the field and plucked two stalks out of the crop circle that he compared to another stalk that he had stepped on when entering the field. The stalks from the crop circle showed no breaks on the so-called "apical knots." The one he had stepped on, however, showed a clear break (see Figure 27). Physicist and astronomer Archie Roy, from the University of Glasgow, who has examined many crop circles, called the whole

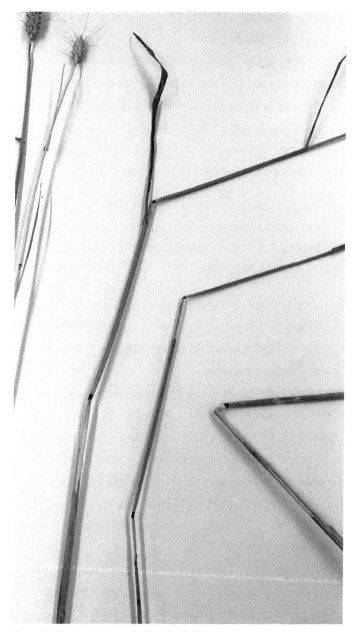

Figure 27. Snapped straw stalks from the Saint-Hippolyte crop circle.

thing "an enormous riddle."[23] Physicist Eltjo Haselhof, perhaps the best-known expert on crop circles, states: "The cause of the burst stalks is a demonstrable, electromagnetic energy. It is the trigger for the phenomenon."[24] But skeptics have paid no attention to his conclusion.

In 2015, British biologist Milton Wainwright clearly demonstrated extraterrestrial organisms in space, despite *Der Spiegel's* statement to the contrary:

> *The organisms must come from space. We found evidence that the DNA is not of earthly origin. If the organisms came from the Earth, they would have to be contaminated with earthly DNA. But they're not.*[25]

In an episode of the *Ancient Aliens* TV show, Wainwright presented his latest findings, which confirmed his earlier statements, and illustrated his conclusions with stunning images of alien microbes.

Years ago, Paul Theodore Hellyer announced to the media that some aliens may look like us and that "they could walk down the street and you wouldn't notice."[26] Hellyer was a serious figure who had served as Canada's Minister of Defense for six years and had sat for twenty-two years in the Canadian Parliament. He had probably thought carefully about his statement and he still stands by it today.

I discussed this question years ago,[27] and my investigation led me to ask: How would we behave if someone suddenly said that he (or she) were not from this world? Well, with a reasonable dose of skepticism and a reserved grin, I would insist that the (alleged) extraterrestrial give me a physical formula, something like Einstein's theory of relativity, that could expand our understanding of physics and our knowledge of the universe. Then I would give this formula to the experts and ask them to check it out.

And that's exactly what happened. Here is the story.

DESERT ENCOUNTER

Frenchman Jean de Rignies (1919–2001) was a trained engineer who lived in Marseille. During World War II, he served as a pilot with the French Air Force. In 1962, he was surveying the dry desert area around what is currently called Road O 1506 in the Ounila Valley in Morocco when the silhouette of a vehicle appeared in the distance. The problem is that the vehicle didn't belong there, because the road hadn't been built yet. Assuming that someone had gotten lost, the engineer and some other men approached the vehicle. When they got closer, they were confused by what they saw—something completely unknown to them that was neither a car nor an airplane. Some human-like beings stood around it.

As the engineers looked on, de Rignies suddenly felt a telepathic vibration in his brain. Then benevolent and friendly thoughts formed in his mind and a strange voice asked about the exact geographical location. As a survey engineer, de Rignier of course knew exactly where they were. So he concentrated intensely on their position and the telepathic voice in his brain told him that they would have further contact. The strangers then climbed into their odd vehicle and disappeared into the sky at great speed.

Many years after returning to France, de Rignies continued to receive spontaneous messages that contained complicated algebraic formulas and symbols of all kinds. From them, he learned that we earthlings are the descendants of extraterrestrials, and that we have inherited all their faults and advantages. De Rignies diligently recorded all these messages in his notebook, and these notes are accessible to everyone today.

Publisher Werner Betz from Groß-Gerau published all of Jean de Rignies's writings in *Riss in der Matrix* (*Rift in the Matrix*).[28] The work is cleverly formatted, with the original French text reproduced in de Rignies's own writing on the left-facing page and the German translation on the right. Although I speak some French, I had great difficulty following Jean de Rignies's handwritten notes, which are teeming with algebraic equations that I don't understand. The formulas purportedly complement Einstein's theory of relativity and give instructions for constructing quantum computers.

The computers that most of us are familiar with today work on the principles of physics that we currently know. Quantum computers, on the other hand, work on principles based in quantum mechanical states that allow even the most complex calculations to be carried out at incredible speeds. The development of these computers was the result of arduous and expensive research. In 2005, the first quantum calculations were carried out at the Institute for Experimental Physics at the University of Innsbruck, Austria.[29] Since then, the development of these computers has moved forward rapidly. Nearly every month, new speed records are broken at various research institutions, enabling even faster and even more complex calculations. The goal of quantum computing is the development of Artificial Intelligence (AI)—which is supposed to eventually replace the human brain.

Jean de Rignies knew nothing about all of this. Yet in his notes, he writes about future computers that work "on the basis of quantum physics."

> *We know that the electron shell of an atom can exist while the electrons reach different energetic levels, which on earth are called "quantum levels."*[30]

Later in his notes, he provides the associated algebraic formulas—just the sort of things I would have asked an alien to provide to prove his or her authenticity.[31]

The fact that a non-physicist could write about quantum computers decades ago and provide complicated algebraic formulas for constructing them is utterly perplexing to me. Does the information actually come from an extraterrestrial? Are these messages part of an attempt to slowly prepare humanity for the existence of extraterrestrials? Is there a progression of information that runs from UFOs, to inexplicable crop formations, to algebraic formulas that lead to quantum computers? Or is this all just nonsense and wishful thinking?

Perhaps. But I have an even crazier story for you.

JOINT BASE ANTARCTICA

Linda Moulton Howe is an American journalist with an excellent reputation. She graduated *cum laude* from the University of Colorado in 1965 with a degree in English literature, then went on to earn a master's degree in communication from Stanford University in California. From 1978 to 1983, she worked as Director for Special Projects at KMGH-TV Channel 7 in Denver. Subsequently, she worked as a journalist for various magazines and TV stations and made a name for herself as an investigative reporter who examined controversial research topics thoroughly and comprehensively. Her diligent reporting had already brought to light several amazing stories.

I have known Linda for several years and meet her regularly at international conferences. We met at the end of May 2019 in Indian Wells, California, at the Contact in the Desert conference. I listened with astonishment and great skepticism to her conference lecture. What she was saying could simply not be true.

In a matter-of-fact and calm manner, Linda spoke about a secret base in Antarctica that is jointly run by humans and extraterrestrials. She insisted that, since she protects her sources, she could not disclose any of their names. So was this all just a fantasy presented by a famous journalist? The next day, I asked Linda for a short one-on-one conversation (see Figure 28).

Figure 28. Linda Molton Howe with Erich von Däniken.

"Linda," I began, "do you want to ruin your reputation? What's up with this story about a secret base in Antarctica where humans and extraterrestrials exchange information and even technology?"

Linda looked me straight in the eye and reached for her bag, which always hangs on her shoulder or around the back of her chair. "Erich," she replied, "I will show you some documents and also use my cell phone to play conversations I had with the scientists and military officers involved. But the names of all these individuals must be kept secret. You are not allowed to go public. I promised that to these individuals. If you make the same promise to me, I'll show you more."

Needless to say, I promised.

Linda got some documents out of her bag and said that, years ago, she had met an Air Force pilot who was a member of the Antarctic Development Squadron. She showed me a copy of a document that bore the logo of the U. S. Antarctic Development Squadron VXE-6, along with the name of a pilot and an award he had received. Until 1999, the pilot had regularly flown a C-130, an aircraft designed for heavy transport in inaccessible regions, from the southern tip of New Zealand to the McMurdo Sound region of Antarctica.

The pilot had told Linda that, over the area of the Ross Sea, he and other pilots had repeatedly seen shiny silver discs flying and that he had photographed them. Linda then showed me a picture. The disks flew between the mountains, the pilot said, and then disappeared without a trace. Apart from the runway used by the C-130s, there was no other runway in the area and the pilot claimed never to have seen a UFO landing or taking off. So where did these craft come from and where did they go?

Through her pilot contact, Linda met the commander of a Navy Seal unit in 2012 who claimed to have been at the secret Antarctic station three times. The Navy Seals are considered the toughest military unit in the world. Their motto is "The Only Easy Day Was Yesterday," and only the strongest individuals make it through their training. This Seal's mission was to protect the secret scientific base in Antarctica. No tourists stroll across the Antarctic ice, but espionage or terrorist attacks were always a threat.

The Seal had told her that, in this frozen landscape, there were gigantic underground ice halls in which alien vehicles were parked. The temperature in these shelters is always constant, and there are characters and symbols glowing on some walls that are not terrestrial. He also knew a physicist who told him before he retired that humans and extraterrestrials work together there.

"How long has this been going on?" I asked Linda. She didn't know, but her informant had indicated that the station had obviously existed for thousands of years— since the appearance of *homo sapiens.*

Well, in this case, I became the skeptic. I believed Linda's descriptions—after all, she had shown me documents and I had heard a conversation with the commandant of the Navy Seals on her cell phone. But I had to question the credibility and motivation of people who would reveal secrets like this. Was this base built for the purpose of preparing humanity bit by bit to accept the impossible?

Then I associated a possible base in Antarctica that might have existed for millennia with the maps of Piri Reis that showed an ice free Antarctica as well as the exact coastlines and islands that are hidden today under thick layers of ice—Antarctica as it existed millennia ago. The connection really got my attention, because the existence of these maps was an indisputable fact.

Then I recalled another indisputable fact. On October 19, 2017, a small space object was discovered by astronomers in Hawaii who were the first to see it using the Panoramic Survey Telescope. The object was dubbed Oumuamua, which means "ambassador from the past."

The object moves faster than any meteor fragment could; it is also a very good reflector of sunlight. The object has been classified as an "interstellar object"—the first interstellar object to be discovered in our solar system that does not orbit our sun. Although the object is now too far away to be observed, Harvard astrophysicist Abraham Loeb thinks it is very possible that Oumuamua is an artificial object that is propelled by a solar sail.[32] This opinion was shared by several colleagues. But instead of breaking out in jubilation, the professional world has maintained a profound silence about this astounding discovery. Nobody wants to get their fingers burned on Oumuamua. Nobody dares to go out on a limb. UFO? Because of this conspiracy of silence, we may never know.

But we have to ask ourselves why the Maya started their calendar on August 11, 3113 BC. What was so important about that date that a new calendar had to be created to mark it? I contend that it was the coming of the gods to Earth from the stars.

I encourage all religions and cultures on Earth today to begin a new, universal calendar. I think we should designate 2020 as the new Year 1.

Why?

Because I believe the gods have returned.

NOTES

CHAPTER 2

1 Krauss, Rolf: "Zum archäologischen Befund im thebanischen Königsgrab Nr. 62," in: *Mitteilungen der Deutschen Orientgesellschaft*, 1986.

2 Frischauer, Paul: *Es steht geschrieben*, Zürich, 1967.

3 Diodorus Siculus: *Historische Bibliothek*, Band XIX.

4 Mayer Burgstein, Stanley: *The Babylonica of Berossus*, Malibu, USA, 1980.

5 Widengren, Geo: *Hochgottglaube im alten Iran*, Uppsala, 1938.

6 Aram, Kurt: *Magie und Zauberei in der alten Welt*, Berlin, 1927.

7 Numazawa, Kiichi Franz: *Die Weltanfänge der japanischen Mythologie*, Freiburg/Br., 1946.

8 Eusebius: *Werke, Christliche Schriftsteller der ersten drei Jahrhunderte*, Band V, Leipzig 1911.

9 Barthel, Thomas: "Die gegenwärtige Situation in der Erforschung der Maya-Schrift," in: *Proceedings of the Thirty-Second International Congress of Americanist*.

10 Barthel, Thomas: "Mayahieroglyphen," in: *Bild der Wissenschaft*, Heft 6, 4. Jahrgang, Juni 1967.

11 Stuart, David und George: *Palenque, Eternal City of the Maya*, London, 2008.

12 Ibid.

13 Wilhelmy, Herbert: *Welt und Umwelt der Maya*, München, 1981.

14 Apelt, Otto: *Platon—sämtliche Dialoge. Kritias und Timaios*, 1922 (Neuauflage, Hamburg, 1988).

15 Däniken, Erich von: *Im Namen von Zeus*, München, 1999.

16 Karst, Josef: *Eusebius Werke. Die Chronik*, Leipzig, 1911

17 The whole story can be read in chapter 82 of the *Book of Enoch*. See Berdyczweski, M.J. (Bin Gorion): *Die Sagen der Juden. Von der Urzeit*, Band 1, Frankfurt a.M., 1913.

18 Kautzsch, Emil: *Die Apokryphen und Pseudepigraphen des Alten Testaments*. Das Buch Henoch, Tübingen, 1900.

19 Däniken, Erich von: *Falsch informiert!* Rottenburg, 2007.

20 *Das Pyramidenkapital in Al-Makrizi's "Hitat,"* übersetzt von E. Graefe, Leipzig, 1911.

21 Ibid.

22 Däniken, Erich von: *Der Mittelmeerraum und seine mysteriöse Vorzeit*, Rottenburg, 2012.

23 Pofalla, Boris: "All unser Wissen," in: *Welt am Sonntag*, 8. Juli 2018.

24 For more on these repositories, see Däniken, Erich von: *Botschaften aus dem Jahr 2118*, Rottenburg, 2016.

25 Däniken, Erich von: *Was ich jahrzehntelang verschwiegen habe*, Rottenburg, 2016.

26 Landa, Diego de: *Relación de las cosas de Yucatán*, Madrid, 1566.

27 Acosta, José de: *Historia natural y moral de los Indios*, Band VI, Sevilla, 1590.

28 Berdyczweski, M.J. (Bin Gorion): *Die Sagen der Juden. Von der Urzeit*, Band 1, Frankfurt a.M. 1913.

29 Fuchs, C.: "Das Leben Adams und Evas," in: *Die Apokryphen und Pseudepigraphen des Alten Testaments*, Band II, herausgegeben von Emil Kautsch, Hildesheim, 1962.

CHAPTER 3

1 *Plutarch: Lebensbeschreibungen,* bearbeitet von Hans Floerke, Leipzig, 1913.

2 Tournefort, Joseph Pitton de: *Relation d'un Voyage du Levant,* Paris, 1717.

3 Kern, Hermann: *Labyrinthe,* München, 1982.

4 Wunderlich, Hans Georg: *Wohin der Stier Europa trug,* Reinbek, 1972.

5 Sonnenberg, Ralf: "Das Rätsel der Magazine," in: *Kosmische Spuren,* München, 1989.

6 Tripp, Edward: *Reclams Lexikon der antiken Mythologie,* Stuttgart, 1974.

7 Schwab, Gustav: *Sagen des klassischen Altertums,* Wien, 1972. [34] *Die Argonauten des Apollonius,* Zürich, 1779.

8 Schefold, Karl und Jung, Franz: *Die Sagen von den Argonauten,* München o.J.

9 Ibid.

10 *Kebra Nagast, die Herrlichkeit der Könige,* in: Abhandlungen der Philosophisch-Philologischen Klasse der Königlich Bayrischen Akademie der Wissenschaften, Band 23, München, 1905.

11 Gaius Plinius Secundus: *Die Naturgeschichte,* übersetzt von Prof. Dr. G. C. Wittstein, Leipzig, 1882.

12 *Herodot: Historien,* zweiter Band, München o.J.

13 Mariette, August: *Le Séraphéum des Memphis,* Paris, 1857 (veröffentlicht von Gaston Maspero).

14 Schott, Albert: *Das Gilgamesch-Epos,* Stuttgart, 1977.

15 Karst, Josef: *Eusebius Werke, Die Chronik,* Band 5, Leipzig, 1911.

16 Däniken, Erich von: *Die Augen der Sphinx,* München, 1989.

17 *Herodot: Historien*, zweiter Band, München o.J.

18 Diodor von Sizilien: *Geschichts-Bibliothek*, übersetzt von Dr. Adolf Wahrmund, Stuttgart, 1866.

19 Ibid, chapter 66.

20 Strabon: *Erdbeschreibung*, übersetzt von Dr. A. Forbiger, Berlin o.J.

21 *Gaius Plinius Secundus: Die Naturgeschichte.*

22 Skonieczny, C. et al.: "Monsoon-Driven Saharan Dust Variability over the Past 240,000 Years," in: *Science Advances*, herausgegeben von der American Association for the Advancement of Science, New York, 2019.

23 Däniken, Erich von: *Die Augen der Sphinx*, München, 1989.

24 Lepsius, Richard: *Denkmäler aus Ägypten und Äthiopien*, Berlin, 1849.

25 Lepsius, Richard: *Briefe aus Ägypten*, Berlin, 1852.

26 Ibid.

27 Kimball, O. Armayor: *Herodotus' Autopsy of the Fayoum*, Amsterdam, 1985.

CHAPTER 4

1 Sulzbach, A.: *Targum Scheni. Zum Buch Ester*, Frankfurt/M., 1920.

2 Däniken, Erich von: *Erinnerungen an die Zukunft*, Düsseldorf, 1968, pp. 35–38.

3 Hapgood, Charles H.: *Die Weltkarten der alten Seefahrer*, Rottenburg, 2019. See also *Maps of the Ancient Sea Kings*.

4 *Kebra Nagast, die Herrlichkeit der Könige*, herausgegeben von Carl Bezold, Band 23, 1. Abteilung, München, 1905.

5 Rotter, Gernot: *Al-Mas'udi: Bis zu den Grenzen der Erde*, Tübingen, 1978.

6 See Däniken, Erich von: *Unmögliche Wahrheiten*, Rottenburg, 2013; see also Däniken, Erich von: *Das unheilige
Buch*, Rottenburg, 2014.

CHAPTER 5

1 Makemson, Worcester M.: *The Book of the Jaguar Priest*,
a translation of the book of Chilam Balam of Tizimin
with Commentary, New York, 1951.

2 *Wonders of the Cosmos, Scientific American* Sonderheft, September 2017.

3 *Are We Alone? Popular Sciences* Sonderheft, New York,
Oktober 2017.

4 *Life beyond Earth?* Special *Newsweek* Edition, 9. Dezember
2017.

5 *We Are Not Alone, National Geographic* Sonderheft, März
2019

6 "Bereit für den Kontakt?" in: *P.M. Magazin*, Februar
2018.

7 "Ist da draußen wer?" *NZZ-Folio*, Nr. 336 vom Juli 2019.

8 Cooper, Helene, Blumenthal, Ralph und Kean, Leslie:
"'Wow—What Is That?' Navy Pilots Report Unexplained
Flying Objects," in: *New York Times*, 26. Mai 2019.

9 *New York Times*/To The Stars Academy/U.S. Department of Defense.

10 "US-Kampfpiloten widersprechen Drohnen-Erklärung
für Navy-UFOs," unter: *grenzwissenschaft-aktuell.de*, 27.
Mai 2019.

11 "US-Senatoren werden vertraulich zu UFO-Sichtungen
gebrieft," *Kopp Report* vom 29. Juni 2019.

12 Dreszner, Daniel W.: "UFOs Exist and Everyone Needs
to Adjust to That Fact," in: *Washington Post*, 28. Mai
2019.

13 Evers, Marco: "9/11 aus dem All," in: *Der Spiegel*, Nr. 25 vom 15. Juni 2019.

14 Costa, Ch. und Miller, L.: *UFO Sightings Desk Reference. United States of America 2001–2015. Unidentified Flying Objects: Frequency, Distributions, Shapes*, Syracuse, NY, 2017.

15 *Der Spiegel*, Nr. 31/1991.

16 "Die Wahrheit über UFOs," n-tv-Doku (Deutschland), 9. Juni 2015.

17 Pope, Nick: Speech from 8. April bei der "Ozark Mountain UFO Conference" in Eureka Springs, AR, USA.

18 Kean, Leslie: *UFOs. Generäle, Piloten und Regierungsvertreter brechen ihr Schweigen*, Rottenburg, 2012.

19 Däniken, Erich von: *Botschaften aus dem Jahr 2118*, Rottenburg, 2018, Seite 31ff.

20 Mack, John E.: *Abductions—Human Encounters with Aliens*, New York, 1994; Ludwiger, Illobrand von: *Ergebnisse aus 40 Jahren UFO-Forschung*, Rottenburg, 2015; Fiebag, Johannes: *Kontakt—UFO-Entführungen in Deutschland, Österreich und der Schweiz*, München, 1994.

21 Kean, Leslie: *UFOs. Generäle, Piloten und Regierungsvertreter brechen ihr Schweigen*, Rottenburg, 2012.

22 *The Brookings Report*. Herausgegeben vom Committee on Long-Range Studies im Auftrag der NASA, Washington, Dezember 1960.

23 Noyes, Ralph und Busty, Taylor: *Die Kreise im Korn*, München, 1991.

24 Haselhof, Eltjo: "Opinions and Comments: Dispersion of Energies in Worldwide Crop Formations," in: *Physiologia Planetarum*, S. 123–125, Eindhoven, Niederlande, 2000.

25 "Is This Evidence of Alien Life Near Earth? Controversial Scientist Says He Has Found MORE Organisms 25 Miles above the Planet," in: *Mail Online, https://www .dailymail.co.uk*, 6. April 2015, Update: 7. April 2015.

26 "Alien Technology: The Best Hope to Save Our Planet," in: *Ottawa Citizen*, Kanada, 28. Februar 2007.

27 Däniken, Erich von: *Botschaften aus dem Jahr 2118*, Rottenburg, 2018, Seite 31ff.

28 Betz, Werner, Vits, Udo und Ampssler, Sonja: *Riss in der Matrix. Begegnung mit einer anderen Dimension*, Groß-Gerau, 2019.

29 Meier, C. J.: *Eine kurze Geschichte des Quantencomputers*, Hannover, 2015.

30 Betz, Werner, Vits, Udo und Ampssler, Sonja: *Riss in der Matrix*, pp. 27–28.

31 Ibid.

32 "Oumuamua: ein künstliches Objekt?" in: *Space. Das Weltraum-Magazin*, Mai 2019.

ABOUT THE AUTHOR

ERICH VON DÄNIKEN is arguably the most widely read and most copied nonfiction author in the world. He published his first (and best-known) book, *Chariots of the Gods,* in 1968. The worldwide bestseller was followed by forty more books, including the recent bestsellers *War of the Gods, Eyewitness to the Gods, The Gods Never Left Us, Twilight of the Gods, History Is Wrong, Evidence of the Gods, Remnants of the Gods,* and *Odyssey of the Gods.* His works have been translated into twenty-eight languages and have sold more than sixty-five million copies. Several have also been made into films.

Von Däniken's ideas have been the inspiration for a wide range of television series, including the History Channel's hit *Ancient Aliens.* His research organization, the AAS-RA/legendarytimes.com (Archaeology, Astronauts, and SETI Research Association), comprises laymen and academics from all walks of life. Internationally, it boasts about 10,000 members. Erich lives in Switzerland but is an ever-present figure on the international lecture circuit, traveling more than 100,000 miles a year.

Except where noted, all images are drawn from the archive of Erich von Däniken, CH-3803 Beatenberg, with several photos by Ramon Zürcher.

To follow Erich's latest work, visit *www.daniken.com/en/* or Erich von Däniken's Official Fan Page on Facebook.

ALSO BY
ERICH VON DÄNIKEN
AND FROM
NEW PAGE BOOKS